Strategies of
Light
and
Darkness

Mark L. Prophet and Elizabeth Clare Prophet on

Strategies of
Light
and
Darkness

Teachings from the Messengers
at Maitreya's Mystery School

Staff of Summit University

THE SUMMIT LIGHTHOUSE LIBRARY®

MARK L. PROPHET AND ELIZABETH CLARE PROPHET ON
STRATEGIES OF LIGHT AND DARKNESS
by Staff of Summit University
Copyright © 2002 The Summit Lighthouse Library
All rights reserved

No part of this book may be reproduced; translated; electronically stored, posted or transmitted; or translated in any format or medium whatsoever without written permission, except by a reviewer who may quote brief passages in a review.

For information, contact The Summit Lighthouse Library,
PO Box 5000, Gardiner, MT 59030-5000.
Tel: 1-800-245-5445 or 406-848-9500.
E-mail: info@summituniversitypress.com
Web site: www.summituniversitypress.com

Library of Congress Control Number: 2002106961
ISBN 0-9720402-3-4

THE SUMMIT LIGHTHOUSE LIBRARY®

Church Universal and Triumphant, Keepers of the Flame, *Pearls of Wisdom*, Science of the Spoken Word, Summit University, Summit University Press and The Inner Retreat are trademarks registered in the U.S. Patent and Trademark Office and in other countries. All rights to their use are reserved.

Interior design: Brad Davis

Printed in the United States of America

08 07 06 05 04   6 5 4 3 2

Table of Contents

Preface		7
Why a Book on the Strategies of Darkness?		12
33 Strategies of Darkness and 33 Strategies of Light		22
1	Separation from the body of God	22
2	Separation from hierarchy	22
3	Isolation and aloneness	22
4	The light of the lightbearers perpetuating the false hierarchy	25
5	"You are not good enough."	27
6	Deprive the lightbearers of the knowledge of the path of the ascension, the light within and that they are worthy of their ascension	33
7	Condemnation	36
8	Flattery	45
9	"You have to be perfect before you are acceptable."	48
10	"I have to do this myself."	53
11	Self-absorption	55
12	The downward spiral	56
13	The lie of relative good and evil	58
14	Sympathy	65
15	Divide and conquer	69
16	Imitation	71

17	Strategic misdirection	73
18	The Fabian strategy	75
19	The "feel good" strategy	76
20	Belittlement—"You are out of your league."	77
21	Mix truth with error, good with bad	80
22	Withhold information	82
23	Create a problem and then solve it	84
24	Divergence from God's plan by small degrees	86
25	The tar-baby syndrome	88
26	Cause the lightbearers to make karma with one another	92
27	The mental projection of indispensability	93
28	Karma dodging	96
29	Delay, indecision and procrastination	98
30	"Messing with your mind"—psychological dislocation	102
31	Discouragement, despair, depression	105
32	The pressure to "just give up"	106
33	Preempt the Brotherhood's moves	109

Conclusion	111
Notes	119
The Chart of Your Divine Self	124
Acknowledgments	128
For Further Study	129

Preface

In the midst of the battle between light and darkness, we offer this book as a ready help for those who serve the light. It is based on the Teachings of the Ascended Masters released by their messengers Mark L. Prophet, now the ascended master Lanello, and Elizabeth Clare Prophet.

The ascended masters are part of a vast Brotherhood of spiritual beings and angelic hosts that join hands with mankind to work for the betterment of life on earth. This spiritual order, the Great White Brotherhood,* works with earnest seekers and public servants of every race, religion and walk of life to assist humanity in its evolution. They called their messengers, Mark and Elizabeth, to be prophets of God and deliver their teachings. *Prophet* means one who speaks for God—a messenger.

Many years ago the masters called for a book on the strategies of light and darkness. While the messengers did not write the book on the outer, they gave us a wealth of teaching on the strategies of darkness and how to overcome them with light, often sharing how they made decisions and navigated life's challenges. *Strategies of Light and Darkness*, a compilation and distillation of some of these teachings, will, it is hoped, give seekers a framework for studying these

---

* The word "white" refers not to race but to the aura of white light surrounding these immortals.

strategies and how they work in our lives.

While the strategies of darkness are ancient, the ascended masters have told us that *they have not changed* since the downfall of the golden ages of Lemuria and Atlantis. Earth is intended to come again into a golden age of freedom, peace and enlightenment. For this to happen, we must all pass our initiations under the guidance of the Brotherhood of light—thus, the need for messengers and teachers.

Lord Maitreya, the hierarch of the Mystery School on Lemuria known as the Garden of Eden, has advised us to know who and what we are up against in this spiritual conflict. He says, "Beloved ones, you cannot fight and win the battle of Armageddon if you do not know your enemy. It is as simple as that. It is not enough to know the enemy. You must know the strategies of that enemy."[1]

The "enemy," or the forces of darkness, has many forms and can exist in the physical plane as well as on the astral plane. Darkness, broadly defined, includes not only individuals consciously tied to the left-handed path and the forces working through them, but also our own untransmuted lesser self. In fact, the messengers have taught that the most important enemy we have to face is the enemy within, our own dweller-on-the-threshold.[2]

For this reason, the messengers have instructed students at Summit University to read *The Screwtape Letters*, by C. S. Lewis. This book is a study in human psychology. It provides a humorous look at some imaginary devils and the strategies they use to trip up people and prevent their progress on the Path. Summit University students are invited to search their lives and see how these strategies apply in their day-to-day world. They begin to understand that it is most often the weaknesses in our own psychology that make us vulnerable to these ploys.

The challenge of darkness should not be feared or avoided, but neither should we go out of our way to seek it out. As we become more and more of the light, the confrontation with darkness will come to us. It is simply part of the spiritual path, even as our task is to be on the line where light meets darkness and swallows it up.

Be mindful that El Morya, the guru and teacher of the messengers, reminds us to give praise to the enemy! For the enemy helps us to develop self-mastery, testing the mettle of our souls and forcing us to grow and mature on the spiritual path.

And don't take yourself too seriously or let the devil make you too serious. Padre Pio and many of the saints had a wonderful sense of humor. Mark Prophet would tell jokes, be joyous and have fun. Elizabeth has a delightful sense of humor. Happiness and laughter are of God and are effective weapons against the devil. (The devil takes himself very seriously.)

As you study these strategies, joyously anchor yourself with serenity and supreme confidence in the light of God to overcome, to transcend. Hold the hands of the messengers. Ask them to overshadow you with their mantles and to assist you, with the help of your own Higher Self, in seeing how the strategies work in your own life and how you, too, can overcome. Your personal victory in the light is of paramount importance to all. The earth depends on *your* ascension for its continuing advancement.

The ascended masters present a path and a teaching whereby every individual can find his way back to God. Their anointed messenger, Elizabeth Clare Prophet, whom we lovingly call Mother, has never claimed to be a master, only the instrument of those who are. Nor has she ever claimed to be perfect in her human self. Rather, she says,

> I am the servant of the light in all students of the ascended masters and in all people. My books and writings are intended to give people the opportunity to know the truth that can make them free—so they can find God without me. My goal is to take true seekers, in the tradition of the Masters of the Far East, as far as they can go and need to go to meet their true teachers face-to-face.[3]

We are being trained as an army of light. And every day all of you become more alert, more apprised of the methods and methodologies of the dark force. And that is the intent of our twin flames—to convey this to you, to make you absolute masters of the strategies of light and the strategies of darkness. You are our graduating class. You are the top ones in the school of life before the messengers. And you will stand out as examples to humanity for thousands and thousands of years to come.
                    Elizabeth Clare Prophet ~ May 13, 1973

Our community of Camelot, then, to me, is an experience of many thousands of years of coming to understand the strategies of light and darkness and how the dear children of God upon earth have been fooled by the archdeceivers. I feel that in all of the experiences that we have had together, this is the one teaching, the sword itself, the two-edged sword of light and darkness, that comes to us by the hand of God, which is ours—and I might say ours alone—because we have seen and lived through so many eras, so many revolutions.
                    Elizabeth Clare Prophet ~ July 4, 1978

Why a Book on the Strategies of Darkness?

Mark Prophet spoke of the strategies of darkness in a meeting with his staff on January 14, 1973, just one month before he made his ascension. Apparently, this subject was in the forefront of the mind of our beloved messenger before he moved to higher octaves.

Mark told the staff that he had begun a book called *Strategies of Darkness*. He did not finish the book, and the assignment then passed to the Mother of the Flame, Elizabeth Clare Prophet. Mark also said there would be many more Keepers of the Flame lessons, even numbering into the hundreds. The topic of many of these lessons was to be the strategies of darkness.

In 1975, Mother Mary said:

> We who know the strategies of the dark ones would impart them to our brothers and sisters below. But the messenger who volunteered to write the book, *Strategies of Darkness*, took his leave in the summer of life, which leaves only the beloved Elizabeth to write oh-so-many books of the Law waiting on the shelves of the libraries of our retreats for the translator, the one who holds the key to decipher the Word of Spirit in the Word of Mater.[4]

The key for deciphering the code, the Blessed Mother

explained, was in the aura of the messenger.

Elizabeth Clare Prophet did not write this book on the outer, as far as we are aware. She told the staff, however, that this teaching is contained in all the lectures and dictations she has delivered. If you listen closely, you will hear these strategies outlined one by one in the ongoing releases of the Brotherhood these forty years.

Strategies of darkness that caused the downfall of the golden ages of Lemuria and Atlantis continue to work so well that the hosts of darkness have not needed to develop new ones. In order for light to win the day and vanquish darkness, we need to understand these strategies and be ready with the strategies of light when we meet them in our daily lives.

What Are the Strategies of Light and the Strategies of Darkness?

The Great White Brotherhood has a strategy for the victory of the light on planet Earth and for the ascension of every single soul of light, and the masters, angels and the representatives of the Brotherhood work to implement it. There is a hierarchy of light dedicated to realizing this plan of salvation.

However, Mark, in one of his last lectures, explained that just as there are "houses of light" on the earth, so the false hierarchy has its own "houses of darkness."[5] Just as there are angels of light, so there are angels of darkness, or fallen angels.[6] Lord Maitreya tells us that the false hierarchy has an entire evolution—all the way back to the one who sits on the throne of the impostor of the Almighty One, the counterfeit throne of God.[7] This hierarchy of darkness works to its own ends.

Maitreya gave us an additional insight: the fallen ones plan not for decades, but for centuries. He encouraged us to do the same—to plan for decades, centuries and the millennia. "Let us see, then, how children of God and sons and daughters working with the angels may also evolve a plan and set in motion the safety measures from the Great Causal Body of the Great Divine Director, safeguards that will put electrodes of the Cosmic Christ in the way of the evildoer."[8] What a wonderful call to make each day.

In the name of my mighty I AM Presence and Holy Christ Self, I call for the plan and the safety measures from the Great Divine Director, safeguards that will put electrodes of the Cosmic Christ in the way of the evildoer.

The brothers of shadow know the Brotherhood has a plan, and they plot against it every hour and every day. They try to preempt the plans of the light, and this in itself is a strategy. Our assignment is to know the strategies and overcome them with light.

How Does This Involve Me?

All the strategies of the dark ones involve you personally. Mark said that there are none who are not touched by them. But do you know when they are at work in your life?

It is important to develop discernment. Discernment is the need of the hour. Lord Maitreya spoke of the three "Ds" of discernment, discrimination and determination.[9] These three "Ds" form a threefold flame of love, wisdom and power.

Discernment	Mind	Yellow Ray
Discrimination	Heart	Pink Ray
Determination	Will	Blue Ray

Discernment is when we know the spectrum of strategies and recognize them in our lives. Discrimination is when we perceive which one is at play. Determination is when we resolve to use this knowledge to overcome the darkness. It will take discernment, discrimination and determination, because these strategies can be subtle. This is why the masters have asked us to study our personal psychology. The weaknesses in our psychology leave us vulnerable to these intrigues.

For instance, at one time or another, you probably tried to meditate or pray or give your dynamic decrees, and before you knew it, unwholesome stray thoughts or feelings came into your mind unbidden, without your consent or cooperation. Perhaps scenes from an old relationship or a movie came into your mind just when you were trying to concentrate on God and feel that sense of holiness. As a result, you felt awful, and a sense of unworthiness began to creep in.

The messenger taught about this in her Summit University lecture series on the book, *Studies of the Human Aura*.[10] She explained that this often happens to the new devotee on the Path. The mass consciousness can play stray thoughts and feelings through your own consciousness upon your four lower bodies. This can come in the form of carnal energies and thoughtforms, even blasphemies, dark thoughts and feelings, and so forth.

It is a typical plot of the fallen ones to make you feel impure and lacking in mastery. In the records of the lives of the saints, we find that many faced this problem. Here is how the messenger instructs us to handle it:

First, realize instantly that these thoughts are not of God or your Real Self. You have to know it is a plot. In this way, you expose the enemy, even if it is your own carnal mind. Do not identify with the problem—become objective about it.

Now that it is exposed, you can be totally objective. You can even laugh at the enemy because you have exposed him, and he now has no power over you, being utterly unable to put you in a state of shock or depression or self-condemnation. The enemy's biggest weapon is taken from him because you decide absolutely to not react.

Instead, you place yourself in a different state of consciousness. Like shifting the gears in your car, you change to the consciousness of neutral gear. This is the state of desirelessness in which you are neither attracted to nor repelled by these thoughts and feelings.

Next, you systematically replace the unholy images with holy ones. Perhaps you decide to see a sunburst of light or violet flame over each image. Visualize bursts of sacred fire on the screen of your mind. Then make the call for all misqualified energy to go into the flame. On the screen of your mind, visualize again and again this substance being dissolved by the flame.

You may have to be persistent and call upon the ascended masters to help you, but you can do it! And in your achievement, you feel a great sense of personal victory and of overcoming on the path of initiation.

You have just employed several strategies of light to overcome a strategy of darkness. And the first step was to identify the problem, a strategy in itself.

What Will It Take?

Mark Prophet says we have been outwitted for far too long. Through the mantles of the messenger and the sponsorship of the Great White Brotherhood, the plans of darkness can be and are being thwarted every day, and the light can win. It will take study and application of the Law and individual striving, as well as concerted efforts organizationally.

You may not realize it, but *you* are the key to undoing strategies of darkness and overcoming them with light. Often, we feel alone and helpless. Yet we have been told this is our key.[11] Each of us is "all one with the One." Remember: "One with God is a majority!"

So What Can We Do?

Consciously recognize the strategies of darkness.
Discern when they are at work in your life.
Discriminate and judge correctly.
Determine to do better.
Counteract them with the strategies of light.

Here Is the Plan

You shall know the truth, and the truth shall set you free.[12] Knowledge and understanding can be the two-edged sword cleaving asunder the Real from the unreal. When followed by right action, the light is invincible.

We have identified at least 33 strategies of darkness that the messengers exposed throughout their years of service. To overcome the strategies of the dark ones, there are more than 33 corresponding strategies of light. Each is worthy of our study.

The battle of light and darkness is like a chess game with

many moves to learn. But once you know the game, it is easier to play and to win. God in you plays the game, and God in you is the victor.

You will find that one strategy of darkness often interacts or interconnects with another. The effects of the strategies also tend to feed off one another and to compound. The resulting pile-up, which carries a greater and greater negative charge, is intended to overwhelm the lightbearer, who feels besieged during a prolonged attack from all directions that increases in intensity.

We need to remind one another when we are in the midst of testing. El Morya, Saint Germain and Lord Maitreya have advised us: Forewarned is forearmed.

To pass your tests, just get up one more time than you fall down. Remember that a saint is a sinner who never gave up.

Saint Germain wants one particular quality from each of us—endurance.[13] Can we endure until the end of our cycles of karma and win the prize?

In God we can!

First, a Word of Caution…

The strategies outlined here are strategies of darkness used by the fallen ones, the false hierarchy and every little demon and discarnate. But your own dweller-on-the-threshold, or carnal mind, can use them against you, too. Your own carnal mind is actually one of the biggest allies of the forces of darkness. The greatest mistake you could make is to think that these strategies might not work through you or that they do not apply to you.

It also would be a mistake to apply them to others and to assume that this one or that one is a fallen one because they seem to fit the description or have outpictured one of the strategies.

"Judge not lest ye be judged" has always been the masters' teaching. These strategies are at work much of the time, and we have all used them or been used by them, knowingly or unknowingly. Yes, there is embodied evil. But the children of the light, through long association with the fallen ones, also have taken on the patterns of darkness. And the fallen ones can look like angels of light until their cycle is spent.

Hence, Jesus gave us the parable of the tares among the wheat.[14] The tares cannot be removed until the time of the harvest. We leave this to the angels who are the reapers. Let the angels sort out who is who and what is what.

We are all victims of these strategies, but we can also be instigators of them at times. We must remember that we all have a not-self, or carnal mind. Our dweller-on-the-threshold can be a "tool of the force," as Mark would say. The messenger tells a story of being caught off guard by the carnal mind:

> I used to hear Mark Prophet when we would make mistakes, when our vibrations would not be correct, and he would come right upon us and say, "You're a tool, you're a tool of the force." And you'd stand there absolutely startled and aghast, thinking yourself this sweet little innocent lamb that could do no wrong, and then you'd realize that when you are off guard, when you stray from the nexus of that cross, you certainly can be a tool of the fallen ones, of your own carnal mind.[15]

Mark explained how this happens:

I also want to explain to you that any person in the Heart Center, any member of the staff, any person on the property can themselves become a tool for the dark forces, either through sickness, through a lack of sleep, through a negative state of consciousness, through criticism of the messengers, through criticism or boredom or any other state of consciousness that is less than perfection.[16]

I would say that the bulk of the world's common-denominator people have basically in heart and mind the performance of good deeds. The fact that they do not always accomplish good deeds but, rather, evil ones by becoming tools of the dark forces is entirely a matter of their own betrayal and subtle alliance with darkness. We read in the scriptures where Eve was also subject to the lies of the Serpent, the Serpent working through the ancient strata of the mind itself to weave nets of subtlety in thought and subsequently in feeling, so that men and women are often driven by these subtle thoughts without understanding the nature thereof.[17]

People become tools of the dark forces and don't even know they're becoming that. And the cure for it is for knowledge to replace ignorance.[18]

So, we may see these strategies outplaying through ourselves or anyone we meet. Our job is to be alert to the strategies, identify them and overcome them, first in ourselves and then in the world around us. We also must make the call and not be attached to the outcome. Make the calls for the judgment, and leave the outworking of that judgment to God and the angels.

Above all, remember that evil has no permanent Reality. The dweller-on-the-threshold is not the Real you, nor is it the Reality of others. Hold the immaculate concept for yourself and others, and the only way you can really hold the immaculate concept is by honest appraisal of the Law. Holding an immaculate concept means that you're holding your perfection in action. The moment you realize you're doing something imperfectly is exactly when you have to affirm the immaculate concept for yourself.

Be kind and merciful to yourself and to others. Place your attention upon your mighty I AM Presence and Holy Christ Self, and love the source of light within you and within others. Love is the key to our victory. All that we do ultimately comes down to love. How much do we love?

Love has many gradations, including the ruby-ray love that speaks the truth in love and does not leave us as it found us. The false hierarchy does not understand this love. This love is the Guru-chela relationship in which the Guru points out where the chela is in error and yet loves the chela with all his faults and imperfections, for the Guru sees the reality of the divine and not the imperfection of the human.

Love is what will ultimately see us through the testings, the intense battles, the drawn-out wars and all that we will face on the Path as we learn to master the strategies of light and darkness.

33 Strategies of Darkness and 33 Strategies of Light

The first three strategies are related, and so we will study them together.

Strategy of Darkness 1
- Separation from the body of God

Strategy of Darkness 2
- Separation from hierarchy

Strategy of Darkness 3
- Isolation and aloneness

The first strategy of darkness is always the separation of man and God. The plot of the forces of darkness is to deprive us of the knowledge of the members of the true body of God, our brothers and sisters in heaven and on earth. The move that is made against the lightbearer is an attempt to cut him off from the line of hierarchy.

Elizabeth Clare Prophet taught this concept at Summit University.[19] She explained that the dark force often tries to make us feel that we are alone, that no one else has ever gone through what we are suffering. If we are unaware of what the saints have gone through, we become isolated. This is a maneuver to take from us the other links in the chain of being, which is known as the chain of hierarchy.

Many other plots of the fallen ones lead into this descending spiral. For example, the demons and entities of suicide usually work to make the one who is suicidal feel alone and vulnerable.

Lord Maitreya also spoke of these strategies:

> The proposition on the council tables of the false hierarchy in this very era is to determine by outer and inner programming that the outer person will no longer have contact with the inner person....
>
> Though the children of the light are not of the origin of the fallen ones, if the fallen ones can successfully cut off the individual's contact with his own solar awareness through the soul chakra, with his own heart flame through the heart chakra, with the mind of God through the crown and with all levels of his mighty consciousness, then they will have individuals who have the momentum of light and karma and evolution cut off from the land of the living, from the realm of First Cause.[20]

Strategy of Light 1
- **Study the lives of the saints.**

Strategy of Light 2
- **Reconnect with hierarchy.**

Strategy of Light 3
- **Be part of the Community of the Holy Spirit.**

One of the most important teachings you can share with others is to tell them of their connection to the mighty I AM Presence and Holy Christ Self, the light within. By doing so, you reconnect them with their own innate divinity and with the cosmic hierarchy of light.

The messenger has explained that the antidote to the attempt to separate us from God is to study the lives of the saints. Because the saints have attained, we also can attain. When we know and love them, we can tie into their momentum of attainment. The saints ascended and unascended form the mystical body of God. The members of the true body of God upon earth are a part of the mystical body of God, the inner church, the Church Universal and Triumphant. It is a mystical name, an ancient name for an ancient church, the inner church of the Great White Brotherhood.

Life on the Path is an endurance test. The question of the hour and all our hours is: Can we endure?

Can we endure during the time of trial and testing? Can we endure through the ends of the cycles of our karma?

It behooves us to study the lives of the saints, particularly the embodiments of the ascended masters. Learn the stories of those who have gone before us. Because they have emerged victorious from the trials on the Path, we, too, can endure and overcome in our own soul testing.

There are many ways to reconnect with the hierarchy of light. It is important to take some time each day to consciously reconnect with hierarchy. You probably know what works for you. Be willing also to discover new ideas or rediscover old ones that have worked in the past. Here are some simple but effective examples:
- Give your prayers and dynamic decrees.
- Meditate on your beloved mighty I AM Presence.
- Take time to connect with an ascended master, with the mantles of the messenger.
- Read a portion of the words of the masters or the messengers.

- Affirm that you are a part of the mystical body of God.
- Refute the lie that you are alone or apart from God.
- Affirm that you are a member of the Community of the Holy Spirit.

Take a moment now to give the following affirmations out loud. Give them for yourself and for your brothers and sisters around the world who may be feeling alone or apart from God.

**In the name of my mighty I AM Presence,
I AM a part of the mystical body of God.**

**In the name of my mighty I AM Presence,
I refute the lie of aloneness or separation from God.**

**In the name of my mighty I AM Presence,
I affirm that I AM a part of the Community of the Holy Spirit.**

Remember also to physically connect with the Community of the Holy Spirit. Seek out a brother or sister when you need help. Seek out others when they need your love and support. Take time to reconnect with community in social activities as well as services and decree sessions.

Strategy of Darkness 4
- **The light of the lightbearers perpetuating the false hierarchy**

The messengers have taught that many churches and organizations claim the victory of the individual for their church alone instead of realizing the victory of all through the oneness of all.[21] For instance, although Mother Teresa was Catholic, the example of her life does not belong exclusively to the Catholic Church. She is an inspiration to many walking other spiritual paths.

The false hierarchy actually uses the momentum and light of the lightbearers in various activities to keep institutions alive that might, in the natural order of things, fade away. False hierarchy institutions can therefore be sustained by the light of the faithful and devoted ones within them.

Strategy of Light 4

- **Consciously withdraw the light from focuses that should not be receiving it.**
- **Do not create a false hierarchy in your own mind.**

Saint Germain has urged us: Be careful where you place your attention.[22] Where your attention is, there is your consciousness, and your light will follow. Take the time to withdraw your attention and consciousness from unworthy focuses.

Ask yourself the question, "Am I giving my light to someone or someplace I shouldn't?" If you ask your Holy Christ Self, you will be shown in the course of events what you need to know. You may remember or become aware of focuses from which you may need to consciously withdraw the light. They can be organizations, places, persons or institutions. Should you need to make a call, you can give the following affirmation:

> **In the name of my mighty I AM Presence, I withdraw the light from focuses that should not be receiving it.**

It also may be helpful to write a letter to the ascended masters and tell them of your concerns and ask for the ties to be cut. Then consign the letter to the physical flame. The angels will take your letter to the courts of heaven, and the sacred fire will then consume these circumstances and conditions as the Law does allow.

In his famous dictation "May You Pass Every Test!" Saint Germain also warns us against creating a false hierarchy in our own mind:

> Revere God and let him take care of the human, and do not create a false hierarchy in your mind, a panoply of all persons you know—some you place on the highest rung and some on the lowest in your system of judgment. And then you seek the company of those whom you think to be the important people who can somehow add to your stature. This is failing tests, and it leads to a great debacle as the house comes tumbling down, which you have built through establishing contacts, associations, being a part of that illusory society, et cetera, et cetera.[23]

Almost all of us have done this at one time or another, often unwittingly. Think about it. How often do we tend to seek the company of the persons we know who are the "important ones"? We should remember that we know not the heart of another. Therefore, judge not.

It is a good opportunity while studying this teaching to read or reread this landmark dictation by Saint Germain, which is published in the book, *Lords of the Seven Rays.* In it, he outlines many of the strategies that affect us personally, and he gives practical tips on how to pass our tests.

Strategy of Darkness 5
- **"You are not good enough."**

The messengers have often warned that the forces of darkness will tell you that you are not good enough.

They will say to you, "You can't be a saint because you

have sinned," or "Because you have sinned, you can never rise again." This kind of statement, either made to us through others or through our own dweller-on-the-threshold, accentuates any low self-esteem that may be present from this or other lifetimes.

The fallen angels also try to make Jesus and Mother Mary and the other saints and avatars seem so remote. We then feel that we can never even approach these blessed ones in likeness or vibration, let alone follow in their footsteps. This vibration can be very subtle. We begin to feel that we are unworthy of giving birth to the Christ Child in ourselves or in our families.

The dweller-on-the-threshold, or the carnal mind of each of us, says to the soul: "You are not the Christ. You cannot give birth to the Christ." We often find that aggressive mental suggestion can be very vicious and can play into this strategy. How many times have we heard the subtle voice that is not the voice of the Good Shepherd whispering in our ear, "Who are you to think that you can become the Christ?"

Ponder your thoughts in the last week. Have you felt this strategy acting in your life in some form or another? There is a divine solution, as outlined below.

Strategy of Light 5
- Affirm that God in you is good enough.
- Study the lives of the saints (they also made mistakes).
- Study the psychology of your soul.
- Bind the dweller-on-the-threshold.
- Laugh at the devil, and don't take yourself too seriously.

The messenger tells of a time when Mark Prophet had to overcome this strategy.

> Some of us become so weighted down by the inordinate sense of our own sin that the sense of our sin becomes the greatest sin in our life, because in the presence of that sin, we do not dare to lift our heads or challenge error or darkness where we find it. We think that because we have erred, we may correct no one else because of their error.
>
> Mark Prophet told me how wrong is this state of consciousness. He told me how Morya told him to come and be a messenger, and Mark answered, "I am not good enough or pure enough to be your messenger." And Morya said, "If I wait till you have become purified, we will lose the battle!" So much for the master's estimate of the length of time it would take Mark to become purified. [Laughter][24]

Mark knew of the work of Nicholas and Helena Roerich and of Guy and Edna Ballard, messengers for the Brotherhood, and in humility, he felt that he was not worthy to follow in their footsteps. The point was, God in Mark was good enough!

The fallen ones denied that Jesus was good enough to be the Son of God. So they certainly won't think you are good enough. Jesus' answer to them was to quote the Psalm of David: "I have said, Ye are gods; and all of you are children of the Most High."[25]

You, therefore, need to refute the lie that you are a sinner and can never rise again. Do not accept this condemnation at any level of your being. Instead, give affirmations and decrees declaring that you are a son or daughter of God. Claim the mantle of your Christhood!

Give the following affirmations right now with all the love and joy of your heart:

In the name of my mighty I AM Presence, I refute the lie of condemnation. In the name of my mighty I AM Presence, I affirm that God in me is good enough. I affirm that I AM (a son, a daughter) of God, and I claim my Christhood now!

Again, we are exhorted to read and study the lives of the saints. They made mistakes, but they made it to heaven! Claim the mantles of the saints and their momentum of overcoming all problems we are facing.

The Importance of Studying One's Personal Psychology

The messengers have said that the devil or your own carnal mind will tell you, "You are damned and going to hell, so you might as well do it all. You are going to hell, anyway." It is therefore important to be able to recognize the voice that speaks within you. The still, small voice is the voice of your Holy Christ Self—your guide, guardian and friend, your inner teacher and the voice of conscience. We know the voice of the Good Shepherd by its vibration and its fruits.

Study the psychology of the soul and your own psychology as the masters and messenger have urged us to do.[26] Understand why you react the way you do. Seek professional help if you are not making progress on your personal psychology.

We are all encouraged to work with Kuthumi, the ascended master psychologist, to help us overcome any deep-seated momentums within our psychology.[27] If you are working with a professional counselor or therapist, ask Kuthumi to overshadow and work through that one.

Also, be sure to go after these momentums with the violet transmuting flame and the calls to bind the dweller-on-the-threshold that opposes you. The messenger once said that she believed it would be difficult to make it on the Path without giving decree 20.09, "I Cast Out the Dweller-on-the-Threshold!" (see p. 116) at least nine times each day so that the dweller will not outsmart us.[28] This decree should be given after putting on the armour of Archangel Michael through his decrees. It can be followed by decrees to the violet flame.

Study also the cosmic clock[29] to anticipate your next tests on the Path. And don't take yourself too seriously or let the devil make you too serious. Padre Pio and may of the saints had a wonderful sense of humor, and Mark Prophet is known for his jokes to lighten up a serious subject.

The devil takes himself very seriously. Mark loved to quote Sir Thomas More, "The devil, that proud spirit, cannot bear to be mocked." So, let's lighten up. Feel free to laugh at yourself if things get too serious. And laugh at the devil and his antics every now and then, too.

Elizabeth Clare Prophet offers us a story from her life in which she overcame the "you're not good enough" strategy. Many years ago, early in her training, she was learning how to run the printing press. Mr. Dean, the person teaching her, believed she could never master it. In his mind, he thought it would lower his station as a pressman considerably if a woman could do the same thing.

Months went by with Mr. Dean running the press as she mostly watched until, one day, he made a mistake in printing one of the pages for a Keepers of the Flame lesson. The messenger told the story to Summit University students:

So that was on a Saturday, and on Sunday all of the members of the church came over to collate this lesson. And when I set up all the piles to collate it, I realized this one page was off. There was no possible alternative to get this lesson out but for me to turn on the press and run that page.

Well, earlier that week, I had awakened one morning, and Morya said to me, "This is the day you're going to run the printing press." I said, "Oh, no, I just can't run that press," and I pulled the covers up over my head, and I stayed in bed. This is a fact. That's what I did. I could not bring myself to go down and run that press even though Morya told me to do it, because Mr. Dean had convinced me that I could not run the printing press.

It's a funny thing about him. There aren't that many adjustments on the press, but the whole time he was printing, he'd be screwing little knobs and making adjustments here and twisting his little screwdriver and using his wrench. And I thought, "Well, I'll just never understand how to do all these adjustments on that press. It's just impossible."

So, I didn't run the press the day Morya told me to, but only a few days later when this crisis arose. And Morya knows that I'm the type of person who will rise in a situation of a crisis. It makes me summon my inner reserves and say, "OK, it has to be done, we'll do it."

And so, with everybody waiting to collate this lesson, I inked up the press, I mixed the chemicals, I put the plate on, I got everything set, put the paper in, all adjustments made, and I said, "Well, here goes, you know, maybe it will work and maybe no." But I flicked on the switch, and it ran, it actually ran. It printed the thing, and it was right in front of me; it was doing this printing and I couldn't believe it. It was like some great miracle. There were no problems whatsoever. It was a perfect print job.[30]

The messenger has told us that sometimes the first test of the day is getting out of bed! In fact, passing all the other tests of the day often hinges upon this one!

Strategy of Darkness 6
- **Deprive the lightbearers of the knowledge of the path of the ascension, the light within and that they are worthy of their ascension.**

The fallen ones want to deprive you of the knowledge of the ascension as the goal of life. You are meant to ascend as Jesus did. They also take great steps to prevent you from understanding that the light is within you. Your soul is the bride of Christ, and you can become the Christ. Jesus never said that he was the only Son of God. He demonstrated a path of personal Christhood.

Each of us in our own way is destined to take that path home to God in the ritual of the ascension.

Strategy of Light 6
- **Share the knowledge of the ascension.**
- **Remind yourself that the ascension is the goal of life.**
- **Apply the Law—the Law is impersonal.**

- **The call compels the answer.**
- **Develop a momentum, and guard it.**
- **Believe that you are worthy of your ascension.**

The ascension is for all who desire it and are willing to work toward it. The knowledge of the ascension as the goal of life must become commonplace.

Take the time to share this teaching with others. Call to the Holy Christ Self and sponsoring masters of each soul before or as you talk to them so that you will be guided as to how much to say and what words to use to reach their soul and heart.

You don't need to give them the entire teaching all at once. Sometimes less is more. The ascended lady master Leto said that if you call to her, she will release to your outer mind the information you need to share with someone who is seeking and in need. She has promised to help us when we are speaking to others.[31]

Have a note on your mirror to remind you—the ascension is the goal of life. Give the Ascension section from the Heart, Head and Hand Decrees:

> I AM ascension light,
> Victory flowing free,
> All of good won at last
> For all eternity.
>
> I AM light, all weights are gone.
> Into the air I raise;
> To all I pour with full God power
> My wondrous song of praise.
>
> All hail! I AM the living Christ,
> The ever-loving One.
> Ascended now with full God power,
> I AM a blazing Sun!

Apply the Law—it works when we apply it. The Law is impersonal and is no respecter of persons. Two plus two equals four no matter who uses this mathematical rule. It is the same with cosmic law. The logic of the Christ mind (the application of the Law) is unfailing.

The Law works if we retain our harmony and obey the Law. The messenger and the ascended masters have told us endlessly, "The call compels the answer." While we frequently relied upon the messenger to "make the call" on our behalf, she often told her staff and the ministers, "It is *the* call that compels the answer. It does not have to be *my* call."

Developing a Momentum on Making the Call

It is important for each of us to develop a momentum on making the call. You can call for Mark's and Mother's mantles as a help in developing momentum. Call to any ascended master to assist you in developing your momentum and ask to be able to tie into their momentum until you have your own. The messenger once observed that the only difference between you and an Elohim is simply momentum.

Make the call, turn the matter over to God and go about your Father's business. It is important to guard the light and guard your momentum, because momentum is cumulative. If you are hot and cold, one day a saint and the next day a sinner, it is harder for hierarchy to answer you until you develop a momentum and some consistency in your habits.

Saint Germain once told us that he ascended because he made two million right decisions. His two million right decisions are all about momentum.

Developing a momentum includes not losing one's

harmony in order to keep that momentum. Loss of harmony or anger leads to loss of light. The messenger told us that a major outburst of anger or discord can cause you to lose anywhere from six months to six or ten years on your spiritual path.

What makes the difference as to the magnitude of the loss? She explained that the difference is how many times you have done this over thousands of years reaching back to the days of Atlantis and Lemuria.

She also asked the question all of us would like to ask: "And when does the day come when the sword of Damocles finally descends? It descends and the karma descends and the Great Law says, 'You have had this dispensation, you've had this forgiveness for all these thousands of years. On this day and this date the Law says that the mercy is no longer given to you. You must now pay the debt of all that you have done in the past.' "[32]

In other words, we never will know when the day will come that we have gone too far once too often, when we have been discordant one too many times. Then the Law will say, "Your time is up. You've had thousands of years to correct this. Now we have no more dispensations for you. No master will sponsor you until you conquer this."

This is why El Morya, Kuan Yin, Mother Mary and Kuthumi have reminded us that if we don't deal with the issues of our psychology, we will not make another step of spiritual progress on the Path.

Strategy of Darkness 7
- **Condemnation**

This is one of the prime strategies of the dark ones. Mark outlined one element of this strategy as "the breaking of the

Christ image."

> Now the breaking of the Christ image in any man is occasioned by someone coming up and saying, "Oh, you've got a pimple on your face," or, "Has your ear always looked like that?"... and it's calculated to make you laugh, almost. It's almost laughable. But it really gets at your subconscious to gnaw at you and make you feel that you're an imperfect being, because outwardly we all have these patterns....
>
> Even the most beautiful ladies in Hollywood and the most beautiful gentlemen ... they have that karmic pattern. That's it, the human race is heir to it, even as it is also heir to its original Divine Image. And, of course, it's the breaking of the Divine Image that they want to do. They want to belittle you.[33]

The fallen ones will seek out any small flaw or imperfection in the Christed one and continually draw people's attention to it. This continual pointing out of what is wrong with someone instead of seeing what is right is the opposite of holding the immaculate concept.

The fallen ones always condemn the lightbearer. They never cease in their condemnation of the child of light. It is the condemnation spoken of in the Bible as the accuser of the brethren "which accused them before our God day and night."[34] We call it criticism, condemnation and judgment. It is a little habit that we have picked up from the fallen angels, and we tend to apply it to others and to ourselves.

The forces of darkness will try to amplify and keep people's attention on every bad deed you have ever done. The messenger spoke of this in a healing service.

> God does not acknowledge sin because his light has long ago consumed it. But the devil will never forget your sin. He will hold it up to you in the moment you are ascending. He'll have across the street your dirty laundry hanging on the line. And you'll say, "Bye-bye!" [Laughter and applause.]
>
> The problem with these devils: they make life too serious for us. They make the deep, dark past some kind of an enormous, enormous problem that we can never overcome.[35]

Their goal is to try to make you feel as though you are a worthless sinner, condemned forever. This is a lie! The fallen consciousness of the carnal mind, the Luciferian consciousness, is anti-Matter and anti-Mother. *E-vil* is the energy veil that cloaks our vision of our Higher Self. It is not real. It has no power.

The Luciferians love the intellectual argument. They have a fascination with the mental, which is the antithesis of the love of the guru. There is a subtle but simple trap they use to get you to hate the true gurus—the ascended masters. The messenger explained this strategy in her first lecture on "Teachings of the Cosmic Christ":

> Without the love of the person of God, you will never quite make it on the Path because, you see, when you accept those grains of sand, dust and condemnation about yourself, the fallen ones never leave you alone. They amplify every wrong deed you have ever done. They hold them up as examples of your unworthiness, and they make you believe that they are the guru speaking in your consciousness—they are God speaking, and you must be forever condemned.

Well, a God who condemns you is a God you will hate. The fallen ones know this. If they can pose as the guru and condemn you and get you to accept the condemnation, then you will hate the guru and will have to leave the guru. You will have to disassociate yourself from the person of God.[36]

The Harm of Self-Condemnation

If you accept this self-condemnation, then you begin to believe that God thinks that way about you, too. And, if God condemns you, then, you tell yourself, so do the Mother and the guru. The dominoes keep falling until, in your mind, your entire spiritual support structure is toppled.

Can you recall an occasion in the last week when you have condemned yourself? It can be subtle. Maybe you thought or even said to yourself, "Boy, was that ever a dumb thing to do." Or, "I did this bad thing, and I'll never be able to look Morya in the eye again." Our subconscious mind records and plays back to us those "tapes that we play in our mind." It's time to get rid of the old tapes!

Strategy of Light 7

- **Do not accept the condemnation.**
- **Recognize it and roll it back.**
- **The human self is never good enough—replace it with the Divine.**
- **Connect with your Real Self. The Holy Christ Self is good enough.**
- **Don't allow yourself to fall into the trap of condemning others.**

Remember Jesus' words to us: "For God sent not his Son into the world to condemn the world; but that the world through him might be saved."[37]

The key is to *catch* the condemnation before it comes to you or is expressed through you. This is when we need discernment and discrimination, because we need to know when it is happening. The condemnation is sometimes subconscious or subtle, especially self-condemnation. We are often our own worst critics.

Saint Germain tells us:

> You see, beloved ones, the tests are flying full and sure. We want you to experience the sense of mastery, of dominion, the enormous pleasure of having finished a day and dealt with that force, that driving force of irritation, and conquered and risen above every foible of the senses directed against your heart.
>
> They would steal your life. They would take the flow of love between us. They would break the bond by any form of anger or outrage. And they will steal from you your sense of worthiness, your sense of the mantle of being the disciple of Sanat Kumara. When they can destroy your dignity and you begin to feel like a moth, then you will also behave like one. And till you regain your self-identity, I must pause and wait again, wondering just how long you will flit around the bulb of these serpent ones who have beguiled you into their auras momentarily.[38]

Here is the answer—recognize condemnation for what it is. Refute it. Roll it back. Do not accept it. You may have faults in your human self, but we are not trying to perfect the human. We are trying to be an instrument for God's perfection. The messenger explained what happens when we attempt to be humanly perfect:

> There is a consistent denial that the individual who appears imperfect, who wears a body of flesh and blood, can be holy. There's a denial that we can be holy and still make mistakes. Well, we can make mistakes and still live in the holiness of God. God can use us, not because we're humanly perfect but because he decides to use us.
>
> There's no such thing as human perfection. If you try to be humanly perfect, you'll wind up in the nuthouse. You're going to make a mistake five minutes from now, and the whole experiment will be over with. God is perfect! God is perfect, and he can use you as his instrument. The more like God you become, the better the instrument.[39]

To keep clear of the negatives, give decree 10.14 (see p. 114) to beloved Mighty Astrea each evening. You can encircle negative thoughtforms with her circle and sword of blue flame.

Stop and give an affirmation to counter the negatives. You can say, **"In the name of my mighty I AM Presence I encircle the thoughtform that I am dumb or stupid or incapable of performing this assignment. In the name of my mighty I AM Presence, my Holy Christ Self is good enough and is acting through me now."**

The fallen ones will never admit or accept your victory. You need to seize the torch and claim your victory now!

In the name of my mighty I AM Presence, I claim my victory now!

The Love of the Guru

The messenger once gave a profound teaching on the love of the guru personally for each one of us. We include it here as an antidote to the condemnation of the fallen ones:

> I have also found that God, in the person of the Christ, has an absolute awareness of the totality of our Real Being and can be simultaneously aware of our human frailties and human imperfections. But God in the heart of the Guru Mother Mary is the immaculate heart who sees only that which is Real and that which is light.
>
> The great quality of the World Mother is that she cannot remember the pranks and mischievous deeds of her children, so she appears to spoil her children. Whatever they do that is not in the Christ, she cannot contain, cannot see and will not remember. Now, that state of consciousness is almost unimaginable, but it is very real. Mother Mary has given me that gift.
>
> I cannot remember the so-called sins of the chelas. When I meet chelas, I have no retention of anything but the reality and the perfection of the chela. Yet, I also have the awareness of that which you might call human imperfection, which goes to make up the human personality and determines why all your faces are different, your postures are different, why you come from different races, and so forth.
>
> These are not necessarily evil—they are the way you are. And everybody knows we got the way we are through the combination of our karma

and our great etheric body, our great causal body. So the guru does not simply love that which is perfect—he loves you as you are right now. God has many levels of awareness. We read in scripture that he hates certain conditions of vice and the evil deeds of the fallen ones. He dislikes intensely certain vibrations, but as for his children, those whom he has created, he loves the child, although he may hate the overlay of consciousness that has come upon that child.[40]

The greatest gift of the ascended masters is the gift of Self—the gift of themselves in the person of the guru. The messenger explained that the teaching is not a teaching without the person embodying it. The teacher is the one who integrates the teaching so that it becomes a living and breathing teaching.

The flame of God is in *action*. We know the teaching by action and movement or interaction with the person. Jesus, Morya and Mother are personifications of the teaching. We can be grateful for the person of the teacher or guru or Mother, because during the dark night of the soul, it is hard to remember the vapory concepts of a teaching. But we can remember a person. We can remember the smile of the teacher. We can remember the love of the guru because it is personal.

We also remember to extend this same love to others. Justina, the twin flame of Victory, teaches us of the dangers of falling into condemnation of anyone:

> And so you see, beloved ones, God sends all kinds of lifewaves to earth. The children of God would be wise, then, not to continue to condemn or criticize the villains of the past or the villains

of the present but to realize that this is one of the subtleties of the fallen ones. For if you can find someone whom you think has greater error or evil than you have, then the fallen ones enable you to keep your attention constantly upon that one, thereby establishing yourself as superior.

Therefore, you walk the earth, saying, "So-and-so is wicked. I would never enter into such wickedness." And by this statement you bind yourself to the eventual confrontation in which you will have to choose precisely between light and darkness in the identical situation, given the identical weight that is upon that individual.

Therefore, unwittingly, by your condemnation you sometimes invoke upon your own head a mountain of karma that is held by that individual. And then you must hold the balance until you, yourself, can pass the test for which you are condemning that individual.

Is it any wonder that those who have light sometimes fall suddenly from the Path and all others wonder?

Beloved hearts, it is written clearly in the Book of Life, "Call no man fool." When you call another a fool, instantly all of the fallen ones who are upon that individual, making him like unto a fool, are now upon you, together with that one's own momentum. And when you have spent many years invoking the violet flame and being on the Path, you are clearly unaccustomed to the sudden influx into your life of so much density.[41]

Strategy of Darkness 8
- **Flattery**

Condemnation and flattery are opposite poles of the same continuum—two poles of relative good and evil. The fallen ones have great personal magnetism and are skilled in flattery and condemnation. The flattery tries to imitate the real love of the guru, but it cannot. It is simply a mechanical interchange of personality. It imitates love, but it does not deliver real love. Flattery also creates sympathy, and it hooks you with a sympathetic tie. We will learn more about that later, because it is another strategy.

The fallen angels and Luciferians can be very smooth and very likable. Mother spoke about a particular false guru and how "likable" he is:

> This man has been described as arrogant, dogmatic, righteous, demanding and dumbfounding, yet above all immensely likable, so likable, in fact, that he can disarm virtually every antagonist if only by embracing the antagonism. He overwhelms you with amenities, lavishes you with attentiveness and good cheer—the mark of a black magician. A black magician is always likable. I guarantee that if you met Satan walking, he would be likable.[42]

Mark had this to say about Lucifer:

> I don't think of the Devil as appearing around the world with a fork in his hand ready to impale us. In reality, Lucifer himself is very attractive. He is just as good looking physically as Christ ever was, and this is the truth. He's a very angelic, majestic-looking being. There's not anybody I've

ever met that I think can look any godlier than Lucifer—if you want to go for looks. Now I'm telling you, I've seen.

But I want to tell you something about him, another thing about him. He likes the same things God likes. He likes good music, he likes spirituality, he abhors evil—do you know that? This is the thing that's going to amaze you. Lucifer hates evil because he considers himself the archduplicator of God. Do you understand what I'm getting at? Well, why does he do it, then? Because the day that he fell from heaven, he was cut off from divine energy. And the only way he can get any energy is to get people to do evil so that he can get their energy.

He does what he doesn't like himself and gets people to do what he doesn't like to do in order to get their energy and steal it. How could a being come from the level of being the highest covering cherubim for God himself and then come right down and have all these forked horns and everything they've got? He only puts that sort of a face on in the astral realm in order to scare people. He scares them right out of their energy. This... is just a form that he puts on. In actuality, he's good-looking.[43]

Flattery is one of the chief tactics of the devil. He may ply you with psychic messages that you think are not psychic because you are flattered by the attention and the message you receive. You may be told, "You are special. You have a special mission. The messenger knows about this mission," and so on.

The vibration of flattery is one way to spot the activities of the false hierarchy. They reel you in with flattery, and then later they condemn you—it's a push-and-pull action of the two. The masters come with neither flattery nor condemnation, but with Reality and humility. In a lecture on "The Mysteries of the Holy Spirit," the messenger said:

> Did you expect to be drawn in and told what a wonderful person you are, the flattering of your personality, showing you how to do all kinds of occult practices? This is what people imagine that contact with the master is all about. But this is contact with the false hierarchy. The false hierarchy woos people by this very flattery and these very promises, and the people that go to them are often of that seed of the fallen ones themselves. But many times it is the children of God who imagine that a master would perform in this manner, would attract students for these reasons. And so, these children of light, caught in psychic traps of teachers who are not of the light, must be rescued. We find, then, that those who really come to sit at the feet of the ascended masters, who come to the Mother, are naturally humble, because there is nothing here to flatter you.[44]

Strategy of Light 8
- **Be humble in Christ, and give the glory to God.**

Do not respond to either flattery or condemnation. Recognize them for what they are, and "be not moved." Be humble in Christ. Give the glory to God. In a Summit University lecture, the messenger explained:

> I always observed how Mark, no matter where he was, would never fail, when someone gave him a compliment, to always say, "To God be the glory." Once you start accepting compliments without making that statement, you are in danger of the pride that goes before the fall.[45]

The true teacher/guru/master is aware of our imperfections and loves us with perfect love. The guru knows who we are, good and bad. Yet, while the guru sees through us, the guru never stops seeing God in us and upholds our divine potential. Elizabeth Clare Prophet remembers that, in her past life as Martha, sister of Mary and Lazarus, Jesus loved her personally even though she was imperfect.

The love of the guru for the imperfect chela leads into the next strategy.

Strategy of Darkness 9
- **"You have to be perfect before you are acceptable."**

The messenger explained this strategy in her Summit University lecture:

> The great lie of the fallen ones is that you have to become perfect before you are acceptable to God, before you are worthy of communing with him or even being loved by him.
>
> Because we have accepted the lie that we can become perfect, the false gurus have achieved a foothold. They come in and say, "You can do this, this, this and this, and master your consciousness."
>
> Why do we respond? It's the swing of the pen-

dulum between our self-condemnation that says, "I've just got to get out of this unworthy state by whatever means available," and our need for flattery. Underneath all that self-condemnation you really think you're a great person, and you're so glad to find someone who will tell you so. That's the pendulum swing of the ego.

Self-aggrandizement and self-belittlement are to the left and the right of the real ego of Christ. By responding to those ego needs, we accept the false gurus who offer to show us how to get perfect. Then we go to God and say, "See, now I am perfect. Now you can accept me." Then the fallen ones would have us go one step farther and say, "Now, God, you have to accept me. You have to accept me because I have become perfect."

Thus, the great subtlety that invades our consciousness on the Path is the attempt to control God by becoming an adept. That is how Lucifer fell. He thought he was so great that he could give God an ultimatum, and God would have to succumb. Lucifer was the original power-mad maniac with a desire to control the Guru God, a desire to become omnipotent through a mechanical perfection.[46]

The fallen ones said, "I am better than God. I can do it better than God. I can run this universe better than God." And they may say it to you, too, overtly or covertly, "I am better than you. I can do this job better than you."

It is important to distinguish between good works done to the glory of God and works that are of mechanical perfection performed out of the ego and not the divine.

Strategy of Light 9

- We are not perfecting the human!
- We are becoming divine!
- Keep changing in consciousness.
- Keep moving—you will no longer be in the same place in consciousness!

Kuthumi told us that the ascended masters do not concentrate upon the faults of their chelas.

> We love your effort, your oneness, your vision, your sweetness and your strength. Do not think that we look upon all those faults that you amplify within yourselves. Do not think that we measure perfection by the little things that happen. These are crumbs. We brush them aside. We look at the whole garment. We look at the motive of the pure heart. We look at the discipline, and finally, we look at the proof that is in the pudding.
>
> And the proof of the pudding is that which lies in your hand as the gift, the work that you have achieved. Let it be, then, a physical, tangible book whereby the children of God might go free. This is what we judge, not the little mistakes—they will be consumed by the sacred fire. But it is the little victories and the great victories day by day that are the milestones.[47]

So the way to overcome the strategy telling us we have to be perfect is simple. Just don't go there! Put your faith in God, not your human self or the human self of anyone else. Don't try to perfect your human self, but become more of your divine self. As Jesus said, "The prince of this world cometh, and hath nothing in me!"[48]

Condemnation and the Messenger

We see this strategy clearly when we look at the condemnation that is directed against our own messenger. The ascended masters do not see her faults. They see the good that has been done. They see the balance held. They see that in her service to God, she, like Abraham, has withheld nothing, laying the Son of God within her upon the altar for the accomplishment of her mission and for the victory of every chela.

In the booklet *A Special Dispensation,* we read the words of one who, even though he liked Mother as a person, could not allow himself to understand and accept the messengership until he reached beyond the veil. When he made his transition and was able to see the heaven-world, one of the first things he communicated was: "Elizabeth Clare Prophet has had faults and has made mistakes because she is human, but she is everything that she says she is."[49]

The ascended masters have told us not to judge the teaching by the imperfections of its messenger.[50] When we first hear of the messenger, it is common to think that she must be humanly perfect. Yet, she has often taught about human perfection and has readily admitted that she is not perfect.

> People like to think that I'm a messenger because I've become humanly perfect. I find it very funny. People interview me and assume that I am humanly perfect. I am not. I'm a messenger because God has decided to be where I am and because he loves me, regardless of my imperfections. That's a big, big difference.[51]

The masters have said the same about their messenger.[52] Both messengers came in wearing their "sackcloth"[53]—wearing their karma. The masters let the petticoat of the messenger show for the testing of the chela.[54]

The self-styled enemies of the organization and the messenger seem to never tire of pointing out the faults of the messenger and the organization. You can find all kinds of gossip and rumors about the messenger and the masters' organization on the Internet, and you can spend years picking and sorting through the astral plane trying to discover what is true and what is not. And that is exactly what the false hierarchy would like us to do.

If you tie into this vibration, it can take you off the spiritual path by destroying your faith in the guru and the Path itself. Instead, we should respond, "So what?" Remember Jesus' words, "What is that to thee? Follow thou me!"[55] Rather than trying to untangle the whole mess, just cut the Gordian knot. Don't go there at all.

Resist this lure by instead choosing to spend your time reflecting on how your life has been changed and enriched through walking the Path, through communion with the masters, through praying with the messenger. Try sharing what you have received. Participating in an outreach or stump or local classes and group activities can help us heal after we experience attacks on our Path and/or the messenger.

Be warned that whether it's your perfection or another's that is in question, the carnal mind is never satisfied. It never says die. The carnal mind, a great serpent, poses as the perfect person. The messengers warn us not to let the human consciousness take credit or think that it is becoming perfect. We are not perfecting the human; we are becoming the Divine.

This teaching on perfection can be put forth simply and endearingly in the messenger's reflection that Mark always loved her for herself.

There is an interesting corollary to this teaching about not needing to be perfect. It's making the mistake of not trying to overcome one's problems but using this teaching as an excuse for not striving on the path of self-mastery. It is as if the dweller-on-the-threshold says through us, "This is the way I am. Mother knows the way I am. Morya knows the way I am. God will just have to accept me the way I am." Saint Germain, again in his celebrated dictation "May You Pass Every Test!" admonishes us, "No louder voice did pride ever have ... glaring at the soul."[56]

Strategy of Darkness 10
- "I have to do this myself."

Sometimes we tend to think, "This is my problem. I won't bother Mother or the masters. I have to do this myself." When we do this, we engage in the lie of non-hierarchy.

The messenger has often taught this principle to her staff. She would reprove them for refusing to reach up to the one above them in hierarchy for help or assistance when needed.

Strategy of Light 10
- **Claim your link in the chain of hierarchy.**
- **Don't be a solitary climber.**
- **Be humble enough to get help.**

The ascended masters and their messengers are here to help us with our problems and can greatly assist us if we call to them and their mantles. Be humble enough to accept help. Life itself is a great teacher of this lesson. We often find ourselves in situations that require us in all humility to ask for assistance from others. God Meru spoke to us of this humility:

> And thus, you see, the awareness of need, the awareness of interdependence, the awareness of mutual responsibility and service is intended to invoke humility. Humility [is] that golden quality that is not puffed up with pride in its own accomplishments, that does not remain as an island separate and apart, that does not aspire to climb the Himalayas or the Andes alone but is willing to work, to walk, to watch, to wait and to feel the rope of others on the Path pulling you upward, of others below requiring your service.[57]

El Morya has told us about the solitary climbers who try to go it alone. The heights of the Himalayas, he says, are strewn with the remains of those who have rejected hierarchy.[58] That is why the ascended masters have given us guides and the ropes and tools that we need. The guides are the masters and their messengers. The ropes are the understanding of cosmic hierarchy and your connection through the mantles of the messenger with your own I AM Presence and Holy Christ Self. The tools are the knowledge of the Teachings of the Ascended Masters, the strategies of light and darkness, and the Science of the Spoken Word as the release of the sacred fire and the sacred Word to deal with all problems, great and small.

Strategy of Darkness 11
• **Self-absorption**

The plot here is to get you overly introspective so that you pay so much attention to yourself that you do not pay attention to the world and its needs. Some introspection and self-examination are necessary and healthy and are to be encouraged on the path of initiation. But it is easy to become overly self-absorbed.

How do we tell the difference? We know it by vibration. Ask yourself, "Do I spend a lot of time living in the past or the future?" If we do spend a lot of time living in the past or reliving the past or living in the future and not in the present, we are not placing our attention where it needs to be.

Strategy of Light 11
• **Lose yourself in service—the path of the ruby ray**

The messenger has given the teaching that the chelas of the masters need to get the lesser self out of the way so that we can get on with our cosmic service for the Great White Brotherhood. The masters recommend that we lose ourselves in service.

Master Morya has given us a way to concentrate our energies on the world situation even as we take care of our personal problems. He has asked us to write a list of our problems on a piece of paper. This list can contain any problems, any concerns—family, friends, loved ones, business, community, organizations—whatever is on our hearts. Before giving dynamic decrees and prayers, place the list on the right knee, put a wallet-card picture of Morya face down over it and hold this in place with the right hand. Call for resolution, and then give your decrees and prayers with fire and devotion. Morya has said he will take care of our problems, leaving us free to focus on our world service with the masters.

Of course, this does not mean that we ignore our problems or fail to deal with them in a practical way. One way to overcome our personal problems, however, is to lose ourselves in world service or in serving others. This is the path of the ruby ray—sacrifice, selflessness, surrender and service. If we serve those around us, we often see others who are dealing with more significant problems than our own. It helps us to keep our concerns in perspective.

If you have not written a list, why not write one right now? In so doing, you will preempt and overcome strategy 29, which is procrastination!

Strategy of Darkness 12
- **The downward spiral**

What happens when you put a frog in boiling water? While it sounds awful, it illustrates an important principle!

If you place a frog in boiling water, it will jump out, trying to escape the intense heat that could kill it. But if you place the frog in cold water and gradually heat the water until it is boiling, the frog, surprisingly, will not attempt to jump out. It will stay there and be boiled alive!

The frog does not jump out even when its life is threatened because it does not perceive the danger. The reason it does not sense the danger is that the temperature of the water rises slowly, almost imperceptibly.

This is another strategy of the forces of darkness—producing changes slowly and imperceptibly by degrees so that no one will notice them until it is too late.

The children of the light are followers of the light, and

they are often too trusting and unaware of spiritual danger. They often prefer to follow rather than lead because many of them have come from angelic bands and are very comfortable following their leaders, the archangels. We find that lightbearers tend to follow others, whether it is in trends in fashion or trends of thought or action. Sadly, they often follow the wrong examples in the absence of the true shepherds. They follow the fallen ones with their magnetic personalities and the reflected light in their auras.

Strategy of Light 12
- **Be alert and keep in an upward spiral.**
- **Create your own profile in Christhood.**
- **Rise up and lead by example—others will follow.**

The answer is to be alert. Pray for discernment, discrimination and determination, and create your own profile in Christhood. Jesus gave us the counterstrategy:

> The example set of the light in you must be a quickening. I direct you, then, to the example of my messenger Mark, who is ascended with me now. This one who lived in your midst did truly have the charisma of the Holy Spirit, which is the presence in the aura of the magnetism of love. That presence became a profile of Christhood impressed upon the ethers of the earth. There are many who walk following that profile today, though they know not that they follow him.[59]

We all need to set an example of light and a profile in Christhood, and by this example others will follow, even at inner levels. The Divine Mother leads up the spiral staircase and up the spinal altar. You, the disciple, follow her, and as you set the pace, others will follow. All souls of earth take a reading of the footsteps of the Divine Mother and her children that are impressed upon the ethers of the earth. Those of the light will follow the path.

While we have Mark's example, how can many others who don't even know of him be following in his footsteps, unaware that they are doing so?

We all know at inner levels what is happening on the earth and who is who. We are connected. We meet in the retreats and read in the newspapers of the angels "the headlines of what Guru Ma and her chelas are doing today."[60] That is why the ascended masters have told us that your example is very important. Souls of light will say about you, "If he or she does it (good or bad), so can I."

You matter supremely. What you do, the example you set, who you are—all this is important to the Brotherhood of light. It is known and read by all at inner levels. Others will follow you and the example that you set. Jesus said that some must rise up and lead by the mantle of their Holy Christ Self.

Strategy of Darkness 13
- **The lie of relative good and evil**

Sanat Kumara has said that the "belief on earth today that truth with a capital 'T' cannot be known ... [or] understood or contemplated or contained by embodied mankind is the greatest lie I know."[61]

The serpentine consciousness says that wisdom is relative, that truth is relative, that good and evil are relative. Beware the false initiation by the false hierarchy of the fruit of relative good and evil. This is the test of Eve in the Garden of Eden,[62] of which Mark Prophet often spoke.

Serpent invited Eve to eat of the tree of good and evil and coaxed her, "Just taste it—it won't hurt you. Thou shalt not *surely* die."

Well, as Mark said, "What does that mean?" Maybe you will and maybe you won't *surely* die? How can you be partially dead? Does that mean you'll be just a little bit dead around the edges?

We face this test of relative good and evil every day in subtle and not-so-subtle ways, and we need to be ready for it. In one sense, we do live in relativity because we are all outside the garden of heaven. Saint Germain said it well:

> The problem we have today in this circle of lightbearers is that there is not much farther down that anyone can be cast in this day and age than to walk the physical octave. And therefore, though you *think* the angel has not bound you and removed you from God's glory by your defiance, it, in fact, has happened.
>
> And yet, you say to yourself, "Nothing has touched me. I'm all right. Look at me! I'm sitting here among these devotees as one of them, but I have my own way of living my life independent of that strenuous path that *some* self-styled chelas have taken to themselves."[63]

The Garden of Eden was a mystery school of the Brotherhood on Lemuria. The hierarch of that retreat was Lord Maitreya. Jesus told us that the Inner Retreat in Paradise Valley, Montana, is the return to the Garden of Eden. It is the Mystery School of Lord Maitreya come again into the physical octave, an opportunity for souls to return to the path of initiation under Maitreya to pass our tests.

You realize that the Mystery School of Maitreya was called the Garden of Eden. All of the ascended masters' endeavors and the schools of the Himalayas of the centuries have been to the end that this might occur [i.e., that the Mystery School might be lowered] from the etheric octave into the physical—that the Mystery School might once again receive the souls of light who have gone forth therefrom and who are now ready to return, to submit, to bend the knee before the Cosmic Christ—my own blessed Father, Guru, Teacher and Friend.

Beloved hearts, the realization of this Godgoal and the willingness of Maitreya to accept this activity and messenger and students in sacred trust to keep the flame of the Mystery School does therefore gain for planet Earth and her evolutions a dispensation from the hierarchies of the Central Sun. For, you see, when there is about to become physical through the dispensation of the Cosmic Christ the renewal of the open door to the etheric retreats of the Great White Brotherhood whereby souls—as students of light who apprentice themselves to the Cosmic Christ—may come and go from the planes of earth to the planes of heaven and back again, this is the open door of the coming of the golden age. Maitreya's Mystery School reestablished in the physical octave is the open door of the pathway of East and West to the bodhisattvas and the disciples.[64]

As chelas of the masters and their messenger, we return to the Garden of Eden, Maitreya's Mystery School, by tying into the absolute good of the ascended masters, their messenger, their teaching and our own I AM Presence.

Strategy of Light 13
- **Be not moved by relative good and evil.**
- **Become the Christ—"I shall not be moved!"**
- **Trust in God, and tie yourself to the absolute Reality of God.**

The devil does not come in a red suit with his tail and horns and announce his intention by saying, "Here I am! I am come to take down the mystery school!" If he did, we would all be ready for that test, wouldn't we? And what kind of a test would it be? God does not always tell us the nuts and bolts of our initiations as chelas on the Path because he wants us to pass our tests and gain our self-mastery.

Our testing in this age is to not be moved by relative good or evil. Heed the words of the prophet, "Let God be true and every man a liar."[65] Focus your energy and light on becoming the Christ. Tie into the absolute Reality in God. Trust in God—God in the messenger, the masters and in yourself. Trust in the God flame in others. Do not rely on the human consciousness of anyone.

At the same time, do not be duped or tricked—ask for the light to cleave asunder the Real from the unreal. Do the spiritual work, and ask God to be the victor in all situations. God will reveal himself in the outworking of events. Call for the binding of the dweller-on-the-threshold of all darkness that is pitted against the light. And avoid the temptation to identify the darkness in others. Deal with the darkness within. Bind your own dweller-on-the-threshold, and concentrate on the light in everyone, including yourself.

The Three Tests of Serpent in the Garden of Eden

Eve had three tests from Serpent in the Garden. Jesus had the same three tests from Satan. Eve failed her tests, and Jesus passed them. We are also subject to this testing in this age. These tests form a threefold flame and are described in detail in *The Path of Self-Transformation*, the second book in the *Climb the Highest Mountain* series.[66] The teaching is outlined here as an example of the strategies of light and darkness.

Serpent was a specific individual fallen angel on the second ray. Serpent said to Eve, "Eat of this fruit. It is good to eat, pleasing to the eye and it will make you wise."

Satan took Jesus to a high place and told him: "Command these stones be made bread, cast yourself down from this place—angels will bear you up (in other words, prove that you are the avatar), and I will give you all the kingdoms of this world if you will worship me (the test of worldly power)."

The tests for the disciple today are identical. We need the relationship with hierarchy, the messenger and Maitreya's Mystery School to pass them. Here is an outline of these three tests and what they mean for us in this age:

1. Good to Eat/Command These Stones Be Made Bread

This is the test of the wealth of this world. This test comes to all of us. Will we compromise for the sake of wealth? Will we compromise our spiritual path and our principles in order to be successful in business? There are many ways to do this—gambling, including on the stock market, a little dishonesty in business practices. This test is about being true to the cosmic honor flame. One guise of this test can be the idea that often comes to chelas whereby they think that they can make a lot of money to help the masters. The chela may think, "I'll make all this money, and then I'll really be able to help the masters."

The lie of the Serpent on the nine o'clock line of the Holy Spirit is that you can't get what you want, you can't do what you want to do for God or for the community unless you introduce human compromise or human dishonesty. It is based on the greed of wanting what you want before the Lord's harvest. And therefore, the phrase is coined, "the get-rich-quick scheme"—"If I just engage in this little scheme, I'll make all this money, and then I will be able to bring it to the altar and present it to God, and God will pat me on the head and say, 'You wondrous, wondrous person you, you have become the saviour of the community.'"

This is a projection—and a very aggressive mental projection—that is put upon people: that they will somehow be rewarded because they bring money to God. And therefore, it has been going on for centuries, and even the Mafia itself brings the money, ill-gotten, to the Church. You find individuals thinking that they will find favor by a false conquering of the physical octave—a misuse of the laws of God, a misuse of the multiplication of the light. And it is always because of an overlooking of the lawful means and the righteous means, not merely to multiply the substance that has become the mode of exchange, but more importantly, the learning of the lessons of the laws of cosmos in the multiplication of the light of the chakras.[67]

2. Pleasing to the Eye/Cast Yourself Down from This Place

This is the temptation to look good in the eyes of others. The messengers never worried about looking good in the eyes of the world. They were never too proud to be fools for Christ. The messengers and the masters chose not to do public miracles as Jesus did. Elizabeth Clare Prophet told Saint Germain that he did not need to spend his precious energy appearing to us or proving his existence with miracles. Instead, she told Saint Germain to save his energy, that we would take him at his word and see the masters in the outpicturing of events. We would apply the teaching rather than continually require proof of the existence of the masters. On August 12, 1979, Surya said:

> The ascended masters' teachings are charged with light. And the miracle we bring for those who seek a sign before they will believe in heaven and the One Sent from heaven is the miracle of the soul converted to light and the path of light. This is the miracle we bring. This is the purpose of our coming. For the gift of miracles indeed belongs to the messenger, but only one we will allow for the proof of heaven here and now—the miracle of souls converted to light.

3. Make You Wise/I Will Give You All the Kingdoms of This World

This is the initiation of worldly success. It is the temptation to say, "I could do all these great things for God if I just...." And the "just" is sometimes the justification. The false hierarchy says, "Let us do evil that good may come"—

in other words, let the ends justify the means. But the teaching of the Brotherhood is that the ends do not justify the means.

One example is that some encouraged the messenger to recruit important, wealthy or powerful people into the activity, thinking that it would do God service and that more could be accomplished. Often, those who would give, but not from the heart, would desire to have control in the organization by having their needs met. The messengers told us that this is not the answer, and they did not succumb to this temptation. Neither should we. God will take care of his organization if we do the spiritual work. We can then be free to do God's work.

Strategy of Darkness 14
- Sympathy

The messenger has said that if the fallen ones cannot get you on any other vibration, they will always get you on sympathy. They get you to feel sorry for them in their plight. But why do we need to feel sorry for them? They have had the same opportunity as we have had to choose the light.[68]

The tie of sympathy is one way that the fallen ones tie into our energy source unlawfully. It is a setup, but we have allowed it. There are many ways that they can get in under your radar, so to speak. It may be through flattery or by giving you gifts with a string attached. Then you feel awkward when you need to say, "no," to them. It may be that they are very nice to you and get you to sympathize with them. Sometimes it is through a flow of tears to make you feel sorry for them and to evoke sympathy for them. And even when you try to set a loving boundary, you are asked, "How could you do this to me?"

The ascended masters have spoken of the difference between sympathy and compassion. We know the difference by vibration. Sympathy is a downward spiral that can lead to a lowering of your energy or vibration. It often forms what is known as a "sympathetic hook," which is a psychic or sympathetic hook that catches you at the solar plexus level. This forms an attachment that you, then, must break lest you be reeled in like a fish on a line. You need to recognize when you are being hooked. Often, your best friend can probably tell you it is happening if you ask and are willing to listen.

The sympathy of the fallen ones and Luciferians can make us want to help them because we feel sorry for them. "Come live with us. Come help us," or, "Let us move into your house. Let us be with you." And, in a state of sympathy, we think to ourselves, "Poor things, we'll help them." This is not to say that we do not help others in need. But we need to be careful about our associations and determine whether sympathy or compassion is at work.

Sympathy can be a deadly vibration. This is especially true when we have sympathy for the fallen one who is in a state of choosing darkness and not repenting. When they are in this state, the messenger says this is no time to feel sorry for them, because your sympathy simply feeds your light and energy into the matrix, and it reinforces that matrix. It then creates karma for you because your energy is now going into this negative matrix.

You cannot be with a group of people who are following darkness and expect to remain untouched and unspotted unless you are living a masterful life with your full God Presence and attainment in manifestation. As Saint Paul said, "For what fellowship hath righteousness with unrighteousness? And what communion hath light with darkness?"[69]

Another related tactic is to tie up your energy by promising something but never delivering. The messenger called this the withdrawal tactic and said that she was trained at inner levels at night to identify it.

> Mark used to tell me these funny stories about people who would promise him gifts. They would come and they'd say, "Oh, I have this marvelous camera I'm going to give you," and they'd go on and on about this camera, and then the camera would never come. And you probably wouldn't see the people again, either. I've seen people promise Mark all kinds of things until finally he'd just look at me and wink and say, "It's a psychic hook."
>
> The way the hook works is a person promises you a gift, tells you how great it is, and so you're left in anticipation while you're looking forward to receiving this wonderful gift, right? It's human nature. So what that means is there's an old fishhook, and its hooking right into your solar plexus, because the person offering you the gift has created in you desire, a desire to receive the gift. So, then, you have a vulnerable point.
>
> Months may go by, and every once in a while, you keep remembering back, "Well, so-and-so promised to give me such and such," and you wonder why it isn't coming, and because of that, you're feeding it energy. They have a tie into your world.[70]

Sometimes a person will give you something and then

take it back, or they give you a gift, and you later discover that there are "strings" attached. Mark called this promise-and-withdrawal technique one of the main strategies of Satan. He described it this way:

> Now, here's the psychic hook. Give and withdraw. People involved in this will give you something... or they will promise you something. They may say, "Well, I'm going to remember you in my will," or "I'm going to do this," "I'm going to do that." But invariably, if they are a part of the psychic hook, they will later let you know they are withdrawing that offer, or they'll never go through with their promise. Now, what is the purpose of that? Why is it being done at all in the first place?
>
> The one purpose of the psychic hook is to tie up your attention, because what you put your attention on you become.... And we have to have our attention on the Christ in order to do anything. If we don't have our attention on the Christ and the light of God that never fails, if we don't have our attention on our Presence, we cannot do anything. All that acts, then, is our human self. We don't want the human self to act.
>
> So, the psychic hook is for the purpose of getting our attention. And the psychic hook is always involved with gifts or promises, one of the two.... Beware of getting your attention on people. Don't look for anything. If it comes, fine. There are a lot of gifts that are wonderful presents.[71]

Strategy of Light 14
- **Understand the difference between sympathy and compassion.**
- **"What is the highest good here?"**

We need to know and recognize the difference between sympathy and compassion. One is a downward spiral, and the other is upward. Learn to see human sympathy for what it is and know when it is acting in your life. Ask yourself when faced with a situation that is burdensome, "What is the highest good here for all involved?" Then, act as your heart tells you.

Don't fall for the psychic hook. Don't be attached if people promise you things. And watch out for gifts with strings attached. Mark's advice is to "always look a gift horse in the mouth, my friends. Anytime someone wants to give you something, look twice."[72]

Strategy of Darkness 15
- **Divide and conquer**

This is probably the most well-known of the strategies of darkness and is considered a classic all-time favorite. The fallen ones pull it out of the box every time, and it always seems to work. We read in *Foundations of the Path*, page 220:

> "Divide and conquer" is a method the negative forces use successfully. Man's propensity to condemn has for thousands of years kept him under the tyranny of negative patterns. In fact, individuals who do the same things they criticize are often the most violent in their condemnation of others. And some individuals who think that others do the same things they do, will condemn

them for it, whether they know it to be true or not.

We need to get wise. Divide-and-conquer tactics work to set brother against brother and to create schisms between people at all levels. They work to foment subversion, dissension and suspicion. Ultimately, the tactic works to isolate, demoralize and break the will to resist. It works with individuals and groups and organizations. The ascended master Alexander Gaylord explains how it also works on a national and world scale:

> Let us, therefore, examine certain techniques used in controlling the masses, one of the most obvious yet effective of these being that which is known as "divide and conquer." Since men have the tendency to take sides, those who would manipulate nations and peoples find it to their advantage to divide humanity and to pit them against one another as a means of controlling the world. While political parties, various interest groups and matters of foreign policy provide the means of dividing people on a national scale, miniature power blocs are sustained even within families and small business firms. Furthermore, the smokescreen that is created through the deliberate release of misinformation through the press and other news media makes it literally impossible for either the people or their elected representatives to properly assess the issues and to formulate sound policy....
>
> We are interested in revealing the fact that behind the plots that pit the blacks against the whites, the North against the South, the East against the West, the poor against the affluent

and the ignorant against the learned are the manipulators who use a stream of divergent ideas to set the brethren against one another as a means of unbalancing the population—pushing them either farther and farther apart or closer and closer together as it suits their purposes.[73]

Strategies of Light 15
- **The unity of the one**
- **Hold the immaculate concept.**

The trick is knowing that divide and conquer is the oldest trick in the book. Don't fall for it—rise above it. Remind yourself of the teaching of Hiawatha in the poem by Longfellow (an embodiment of our dear Mark):

All your strength is in your union.
All your danger is in discord.

Don't listen to or spread gossip and rumors about others. If you have a problem with a brother or sister on the Path, seek to resolve it directly with them. Avoid taking sides in an issue if possible, but do not compromise your honor and integrity. Don't let the wedges of darkness of the fallen ones create distrust or suspicion. Instead, strive to hold the immaculate concept for yourself and for others. Ask Mother Mary to help you do this. At the same time, keep your eyes and heart open.

Strategy of Darkness 16
- **Imitation**

The fallen ones have long ago used up their own light and have to obtain it from others in order to exist. They can only imitate the light. There is nothing original about them.

Because there is no originality, they have to steal to get what they want—the light that the lightbearers have. This they do by imitation. The best example of this strategy of imitation is the false hierarchy impostor.

There are false hierarchy impostors of the ascended masters, the messengers, even the false hierarchy impostors of you and your twin flame. The false hierarchy impostor comes pretending to be the true master or the true disciple or the true messenger. They imitate the behavior of the one they pretend to be, hoping that the students of the light will not notice the difference. Often, the imitation is so uncannily close to the real thing that the lightbearer does not detect the subtle difference at first.

A related tactic is to try to convince chelas that the ascended masters have changed their names or the locations of their etheric retreats. This is designed to get you to focus your energy on a being or a place that should not be receiving it, thus diverting your attention from the true master or the true retreats of light. To learn more about the protection of the Brotherhood's focuses of light and the impersonators of the ascended masters, see *The Path of Self-Transformation*.[74]

We have recently observed the founding of another movement that has attempted to closely imitate this movement. If we study the false hierarchy and the moves they make, it soon becomes obvious what their strategies are, and we are no longer fooled by them.

Strategy of the Light 16
- **Discernment**

To overcome this strategy we need to develop discernment. The truth is always there if we are willing to see it. Call to the All-Seeing Eye of God, beloved Cyclopea, Elohim of the Fifth Ray, to cleave asunder the Real from the unreal so that you can see the truth or the error of a situation. Beloved Lanello asked us to give the decree to Cyclopea (see p. 117) frequently, even once a week if we could. It will greatly aid us in developing the gift of discernment.

It also is important not to make quick assessments of situations and persons or be too quick to enter into a relationship with them. Maitreya says that we are all too quick to assume that this or that person is of the light.[75] Ask your Holy Christ Self and the masters to show you the fruit of a situation or a person. If you wait, God will show you what you need to see. Ask also for the lightbearers to see clearly and not be taken in by the false hierarchy and their impostors.

Strategy of Darkness 17
- **Strategic misdirection**

This tactic uses a decoy to throw you off the Path and take you away from where you need to be. Often, the aim is to get you entangled in minor things to tie up your time and remove you from the real battle. While you were busy swatting mosquitoes, the bear has entered your tent.

The messenger gave an example: You are attending a school board meeting where the whole evening has been spent on deciding the color of the classrooms. Then, when everyone is done with that topic and packing up to go home, the real agenda is brought up—a new curriculum. By this time, everyone is too tired to deal with it, or half the people attending the meeting have already left.

There are many variations on this theme. It could be

that you are meant to be at a certain place on the Path, but a minor detour takes you off the real Path for some time. It does require attunement to know where you should be.

Strategy of Light 17
- See the big picture.

It is important to stay on track and on target with the objectives of the Brotherhood and to pick our battles. Do not choose to engage in every good cause that comes along to divert your attention, but keep your eye on the goal. Focus on the light. Direct the light into the situations you are facing. Ask for guidance as to where to place your attention.

The key is looking at the big picture. Keep going back to the goals and the overall aim of the situation. Ask yourself, "What is really important here? What is the highest good? The highest priority?" As the messenger explains:

> We will not compromise our witness. We are at the forefront of that witness, and we will do whatever is necessary. But there is no reason for me to go out and launch an attack on every situation of darkness. The far greater strategy of light is to flood out the emanation of the sun with such intensity that when it hits, the people of light follow its warmth. The people of darkness receive the ruby ray, and we go marching on. We have to live in this world. We have to be extremely careful, and the light will work for us. You see, going in and attacking is the same idolatry as thinking that you are the teacher or you are the one who is going to bring about the judgment.[76]

Pallas Athena also cautions us to be led by God in choosing which challenges to take up:

> The hierarchy of heaven is actually quite complex, and when you see how accurately we keep the record, it may serve to jostle you just enough until you will decide to remember why discretion is the better part of valor! You will not then be so eager to pick up the gauntlet when some thoughtless soul throws it down. Far from becoming lacking in courage or taking a stand for the light, you will find that your stand is being taken for you by God himself, and that you are beginning to respond more and more to the reins of light that ushered all of the ascended masters into the victory of the ascension.[77]

Strategy of Darkness 18
- **The Fabian strategy**

The Fabian strategy is a simple tactic, and it is related to the previous strategy of strategic misdirection. Fabius was a Roman general who marched his army around and around, just out of reach of the enemy. He was known as the "delayer" from his tactics in the war against Hannibal. He cut off Hannibal's supplies, harassed him incessantly and did everything except engage him in battle. He had a few skirmishes, but mostly he just wore down the enemy by posturing before them and by seeming intimidation.[78]

The technique in the Fabian strategy is simply to attempt to wear out the forces of light through endless minor skirmishes.

Strategy of Light 18
- **Keep your eye on the goal.**
- **Keep your eye on Mighty Victory.**

To deal with this strategy, again, keep your eye on the big picture. Keep your eye on the goal and on the victory at hand. Do not be diverted by diversionary tactics or attempts to wear down your energy. Do not be tempted to engage in battle at every turn of the tide or trick of the false hierarchy. Stay centered, and enter the battle on your own terms, if possible.

Saint Germain says, "He who has the greater sense of victory will win!"[79] Note that he did not say that the one who wins is the one with the best army or the best weapons or the best tactics or the best software or the most funds!

Remember to claim your victory and give the calls to Mighty Victory.[80]

Strategy of Darkness 19
- **The "feel good" strategy**

This strategy is very simple. "If it feels good, it must be right."

Strategy of Light 19
- **Know the Law of God, and obey it.**

The keys to overcoming this strategy are to develop discernment, to know the Law of God and to obey the Law of God.

After Jesus had been fasting for forty days, it would probably have felt very good to have some bread to eat, but he refused Satan's temptation to turn the stones into bread. His knowledge of the Law of God and his commitment to that Law enabled him to pass the test.

Remember that our "feelings" are not always a reliable guide. We have untransmuted substance in the emotional body and electronic belt. As these records come up for transmutation, they may create very strong attractions and feelings that could lead us way off the Path if we followed them.

This is why Morya and the masters have asked us to bond to our Holy Christ Self. Enter into communion with your Holy Christ Self, and learn to recognize the voice of your Christ Self as it speaks to you with the still, silent voice in the center of your heart. Fast and pray, and ask to be shown your next step on the Path.

Strategy of Darkness 20

- **Belittlement—"You are out of your league."**

Mark Prophet explained that belittlement is one of the chief tools of the sinister force:

> I should give you one of the chief tactics of the sinister force for your protection in the days ahead of us, namely the process of belittlement.
>
> They have a very definite intent to demean the character of everyone, and the lower you are, probably, the less energy they will spend—in the sense of being low, I mean if your position is less important, they aren't going to spend as much time with you. But if your position is important, the more it becomes important, the more they'll try belittlement. And the belittlement tactics are very gross on their part and so subtle that they take advantage of existing situations, and they will belittle you on every occasion that they get the chance to do so.

> Now, this belittlement will take several forms. In some cases it is a matter of revolving. In other words, you may be lying in bed at night or in the morning. You wake up, and they will project at you a replay of what you have done in the past. This may be in the near past or in the far past. And it usually is a belittling circumstance of some kind, something you did or something you did that someone criticized you for.... It may not have been wrong even, in all cases, but someone thought it was wrong.
>
> This is one of their particular specific subtleties, to have people find fault with or criticize you. And it was either for something you did or for nothing you did. Sometimes they criticize you just for existing....
>
> Belittlement is one of the chief means by which people lose their sense of worth. The real purpose of the dark forces is to make people feel that they are not worthy of doing God's will or that their whole personality is not worthy.[81]

Sometimes the message is that "the little guys should not do what the big guys do." In other words, you are simply a child of the light, and you should not be attempting to do those things that the important people do—take on positions of responsibility or leadership—things that the fallen angels in their pride think that only they can do. The strategy is to convince you that you are "out of your league."

This strategy ties in with condemnation, and the force can use it in many ways. For example, when you begin a new job or project, the force may try to make you feel as if you do not know what you are doing, as if you are not qualified, as if you do not have a right to be doing it and as if someone else could do it better.

Strategy of Light 20
- **Be humble before God and positive to the world.**

As we read each Sunday in the Sacred Ritual, "Keep me humble before thee, positive to the world."[82] This is an excellent counterstrategy to deal with the projection of belittlement—the perfect counterbalance of humility and the positive mental attitude. Be humble before your God who knows your faults but chooses to consider the good that you have done and holds the immaculate concept for you. At the same time, be positive and confident as you go out into the world representing God and the masters. The messenger has said:

> Now our brother, friend, saviour, master and healer Jesus Christ thought it not robbery to make himself equal with God.[83] This is because he recognized he was the issue of God. Jesus is the wayshower. We must understand: not I, but God in me. We don't claim divinity for the outer human, limited self. We claim that the divine spark in our heart and the mighty I AM Presence is our God with us and that God made us to be his instruments, his vessels, his vehicles, to be the Holy Grail we have quested.
>
> We are intended to be the vessel of God, ever humble, ever conscious of our inadequacies but aware of God's presence in us that is the all-power to deal with the world equation today, with nuclear war and plague and conditions that

defy the individual. They are giant conditions unless you have a giant God, the Almighty, with you to solve them.[84]

Again, we need to be practical and not enter in where angels fear to tread. If advice is offered to us, we can listen and weigh that advice in our hearts, no matter where it comes from. We do need to consider the source and know that pure water does not flow from a muddied stream. Then again, do not necessarily disregard the advice outright just because it comes from a source we do not like. The masters can also send us messages through different sources. Morya says, "If the messenger be an ant, heed him." Elizabeth Clare Prophet tells us, "I have received many ant messengers in my time."

Strategy of Darkness 21
- **Mix truth with error, good with bad.**

The strategy of mixing truth and error is common, and examples abound. The most obvious is that false hierarchy teachings always blend truth and error in a potent mix designed to bring down the children of the light.

For instance, the false hierarchy might release teachings that are 70 or even 90 percent accurate. The students of the light recognize the element of truth in the teaching and mistakenly assume that all of it is truth. The teaching, then, hooks the student, and while their defenses are down, they take in the error along with the truth. Later, it is hard to determine what is truth and what is error, and the student can be led off the spiritual path by the erroneous concepts implanted in the teaching.

This potential for truth and error to be intertwined is one of the reasons the ascended masters sponsored their messengers to release their teachings. The mantle of messenger is what ensures the accuracy of the teaching.

There is another variation on this strategy. The fallen angels themselves sometimes do good deeds. This might seem strange, but consider the advantages of this tactic. The good deed gives them the legitimacy they need to be taken seriously. Their attempt to disguise themselves as children of the light will be more convincing. The child of light will then say to himself, "This person can't be that bad—look at all the good he does."

The good deeds also enable the fallen ones to balance karma and to make good karma and thus prolong their existence. The child of the light, then, owes the fallen ones a debt of gratitude.

Strategy of Light 21
- **Don't be moved by human goodness or human badness.**

Do not be moved by human goodness or human badness. This is the strategy of Lanello: "I shall not be moved!"[85] Stand back and watch the workings of God in the course of events. By and by, people reveal who they are.

Pray also for discernment and understanding. If you are not sure what forces are at play in a certain situation, give the decree to beloved Cyclopea to show the truth or error of the situation, and wait until God reveals the answer or reveals himself in the outworking of events. Ask to be shown the fruits. "By their fruits ye shall know them."[86]

Don't try to figure out which people are the lightbearers and which are not, but be guided by principle. Don't get tied to anyone's outer self, but help everyone to do the right thing. The messenger has told us:

We have to be loyal to principles, know people by their fruits and know what the masters have said. The masters often use even the Luciferians and their robot creation to achieve their ends—if they will espouse the causes of the masters so they can make the good karma of espousing those causes. The great hope of the robot creation is, if they do serve and actually become good people, they can earn a threefold flame, and they can be endowed with the threefold flame and have the opportunity to enter the path of salvation.

When it comes right down to it, there is hope for everyone on earth. There's hope even for the dyed-in-the-wool Luciferian who says, "I'll never surrender," because he may very well surrender under the influence of the lightbearers. So there's no point in going around saying that these are the good guys and these are the bad guys, because, until it's over, it's all relative, and at any particular moment, we may polarize people for the light by our decrees, by our example, by our actions. [87]

Strategy of Darkness 22
- **Withhold information**

The devil uses this strategy all the time. He does not tell you what he's doing or even that he is the devil. Others can use this strategy by not giving you the full picture or the complete information you need to do your work.

The message here is clear: "I have secret knowledge that you don't have." Sometimes just the inference that there may be secret knowledge is meant to intimidate. Or there may be the actual withholding of information that is needed to get the work done. This strategy in all of its forms can frustrate plans, create schisms and divisions or simply intimidate.

Strategy of Light 22
- Call to K-17 and Cyclopea to expose that which is hidden.
- Get in the driver's seat.
- Find out what you need to know to get the job done.
- Work around it if you have to.

Call to the ascended masters to reveal to you the strategies of light and darkness. You can ask for that which is hidden to be revealed. Lanello works closely with the ascended master K-17 of the Cosmic Secret Service to expose strategies and reveal that which is hidden. Decree 50.05 to beloved Cyclopea will always reveal results in God's time and God's cycles.

When receiving an assignment or working on a project, ask for all of the information and details that you need to get the work done. Get into the driver's seat yourself whenever possible, and stay on top of the project if it is assigned to you. This does not mean that you do not delegate when appropriate or do not allow others in the team to do their jobs. You can ask others for reports or updates that keep you in the loop. If information is not forthcoming, try to work around it to get the job done.

If you are assigning someone to a project, keep in touch with them and make sure that they have all the information and tools at hand to get their work done. Observe yourself to make certain that you, yourself, are not withholding information.

The motto of the Keepers of the Flame Fraternity is to know, to dare, to do and *to be silent*. An important corollary to this strategy is to not tell everything there is to know about an important project if it isn't necessary for people to have all the details. In this way, you can protect and maintain the security of the projects you are doing for the Great White Brotherhood.

As Kuthumi has instructed us, work with those souls with whom you have an ascended master mind alliance and whom you can trust. But do not assume that everyone you meet has the best interests of your projects at heart—jealousy, impure motives or even just their thoughts that your project can never work can create a negative spiral that can pull down your project.

Therefore, do not share all of the details of the work you are doing until the time comes for it to be revealed. There are times when it is necessary to hold your projects "in alchemy" until they are completed. Do this to protect the precipitation of your projects, but take care that you don't use this as an excuse to manipulate or control others or make them dependent on you.

Strategy of Darkness 23
- **Create a problem and then solve it.**

This ingenious strategy shows the depths of the serpentine mind and serpentine thinking that is simply foreign to the child of the light. The fallen ones create a problem and then step in to solve the very problem they have created. In this way, they become the false saviour or the false Christ. This enables them to gain control and take over a situation no one else seems able to solve.

If this strategy is done well from the perspective of the dark ones, the problems will just simmer and go on forever so that they are always needed as the "saviour." One example is the manipulation of the economy by the power elite and the international bankers. Periodically, their actions have caused economic problems and crises—inflation, recessions, currency crises, and so on. Each time, they have stepped in with a solution that has resulted in more power and control in their hands.[88]

Another example of this strategy is portrayed in the movie, "It's a Wonderful Life," Mark Prophet's favorite film. In the story, greedy banker Mr. Potter steals money from George Bailey's savings and loan, causing a financial crisis there. Faced with ruin and scandal, George is forced to turn to Mr. Potter for help. Mr. Potter is only too glad to point out to him that according to his life insurance policy, he's worth more dead than alive. With George out of the way, Mr. Potter could run the town. An angel is sent to intervene as George stands on a bridge, ready to take his own life.

Strategy of Light 23
- **Trust in God.**
- **Do not look for human saviours.**

Again, the need of the hour is discernment. Trust in God for solutions to problems, and do not look for the human saviour. Solutions may come through others, so trust in the God in all. Watch as problems are being created, and discern the patterns of light and darkness being outpictured in the course of events. Do the spiritual work, and ask for the ascended masters to intercede to bring forth the God-solution to a problem.

Strategy of Darkness 24
- **Divergence from God's plan by small degrees**

This strategy has been described as the "salami technique"—thin slices are taken off one at a time until, eventually, the whole salami has been shaved away. It is an effective strategy that is subtle and insidious.

You can see this very clearly in popular culture. Think of the movies, music and art of the early twentieth century, and compare it with the worst of what we see today. What we have now is so much worse that it would never have been accepted if they had tried to introduce it all at once. Instead, things deteriorated by inches over time, and today, for instance, we have media executives talking openly about pushing the limits each year on what they show on TV and in movies.

The fallen ones simply whittle away at an issue or a situation, and when the lightbearers have their backs turned, they shave off another slice. Often, the intent is never even declared.

This strategy has many applications in the world of form. The message for those of the light is that small compromises can take you a long way off the Path. Sanat Kumara explains the ultimate importance of this teaching:

> Most blessed and beloved ones, you know that I have come to anchor within you the blueprint of the fiery destiny of the 144,000. You understand that in the mathematics of science in a space age, a miscalculation by a fraction may result in being millions of miles off target.
>
> I bring you, then, the awareness of your responsibility and accountability in accepting the

burden of light. Every battle that was ever lost, that resulted in the loss of worlds upon worlds has come from seemingly minor episodes, minor weaknesses, subtle intrusions on the part of individuals who felt that they were not supremely important. They felt that someone else would carry the load, that their betrayal in defending personality and their compromise would surely not result in the death of a soul or a world.[89]

Strategy of Light 24
- Hold the line.

Awareness-action is the key. Once aware, we need to hold the line. Do not compromise when it is important and when principles are involved. Eternal vigilance is the price of freedom. We need watchmen on the wall of the LORD. On behalf of our brothers and sisters, we need to sound the alarm when our precious liberties are being eroded or removed slowly and subtly.

Look at the big picture. If things are moving in the wrong direction, you may need to take a stand, even if it looks like this one point is not all that significant. At the same time, be balanced and reasonable. Don't be fanatical about insignificant details.

The Brotherhood of light can use this strategy, too! We use this approach on many problems in the spiritual and physical realms. For example, we don't transmute our karma all at once but keep working at it, day by day. Each day we can take another slice until we eventually reach the 100 percent mark. We use the same approach when we work on the astral belt of the planet: each day we can remove another layer by our calls.

But remember, the day of final victory will come. Don't let this strategy be an excuse to procrastinate your victory or not charge with the full fire of your being when it is needed.

Strategy of Darkness 25
- **The tar-baby syndrome**

The story of the tar baby is taken from folklore and the Uncle Remus stories. Brer Fox made what he called a tar baby and put it in the road where Brer Rabbit would see it. The result was predictable. Brer Rabbit spoke to the tar baby, but it would not answer. The rabbit got mad at it, struck the tar baby and his hand got stuck on the tar. This made him even madder, and he struck the tar baby again with the other hand, which got stuck, too. Then he kicked it, trying to make it let go of him. Brer Rabbit was literally stuck hand and foot!

The fallen ones often use this tactic. They try to manipulate us into getting mad at them or reacting to them. When we lash out at them, physically or in other ways, we create karma with them. Instead of turning the other cheek as Jesus taught, we become increasingly bound or tied to them through karmic entanglements.

It is easy to see why the masters want us to control our anger and our emotions. Anger can be an open door to tie us to the fallen ones for lifetimes. We stick to them and they stick to us, and we are all bound together until we can forgive and seek forgiveness and balance the karma we have made with them.

Strategy of Light 25
- **Take an objective view of the battles you face.**
- **Remember that it is not personal.**

Strategies of Light and Darkness

- **Forgiveness**
- **Pick your battles, and let God do the work.**
- **Remember Jesus' teaching to turn the other cheek.**

Again, you need to pick your battles. Do not try to take on everything at once. Step back and take an objective view of the situation and the tests involved. Let God do the work. God in you is the doer.

The greatest key is the Sermon on the Mount:

> Ye have heard that it hath been said, An eye for an eye, and a tooth for a tooth:
>
> But I say unto you, That ye resist not evil: but whosoever shall smite thee on thy right cheek, turn to him the other also.
>
> And if any man will sue thee at the law, and take away thy coat, let him have thy cloak also.
>
> And whosoever shall compel thee to go a mile, go with him twain.
>
> Give to him that asketh thee, and from him that would borrow of thee turn not thou away.
>
> Ye have heard that it hath been said, Thou shalt love thy neighbour, and hate thine enemy.
>
> But I say unto you, Love your enemies, bless them that curse you, do good to them that hate you, and pray for them which despitefully use you, and persecute you;
>
> That ye may be the children of your Father which is in heaven.[90]

This is the key to avoid making karma with the fallen ones and those who would maliciously or ignorantly seek to provoke you into making karma with them.

Remember the words of Jesus to Peter: "What is that to thee? Follow thou me!"[91] Call upon the law of forgiveness. Send forgiveness to those you have wronged and those who have wronged you. Ask for the violet flame to go to those to whom you are karmically tied to dissolve those karmic ties.

Remember not to take these things personally. Work on any momentums of anger and on your personal psychology. Saint Germain says that before you get angry, give "Count-to-Nine Decree," by Cuzco. (See p. 113.)

Learn to set loving boundaries, and stay centered in your own Christ Self. Be true to your own standards or principles. Take an objective view of the challenges and tests that you face, no matter who they come through.

And don't fall into the trap of trying to identify who is or who is not a fallen one. It really doesn't matter. Treat each person you meet as though he or she is the Christ in manifestation, and you will not create more negative karma.

But what do you do if you think you may be face-to-face with a fallen one? The trick is to see each person as Krishna, Lord Maitreya or whichever manifestation of God comes most easily to you. The messenger taught us:

> In that instant you have a cosmic awareness of yourself going through this entire exercise of loving the Christ Self of everyone and of specific people personally. It's very important to do where you have a block to the understanding of the God behind the individual.
>
> Sometimes we may suspect, especially regard-

> ing media personalities or government figures, that we're dealing with someone who has very little light or not much God-stuff in them. And so, if you fear that this is a person where there is not a God flame, it doesn't matter, because you are communicating with the Universal Christ.
>
> It is a wonderful thing to see and know and commune with Lord Maitreya personally, wherever you think that there may be a fallen one or someone who is simply out of alignment with the cosmic scheme. You talk to Lord Maitreya, you give Maitreya intense love, and the first thing you know, that person, lo and behold, in spite of himself, is carrying out the will of God because of the intense immaculate vision of your being that the only thing that is real about anyone is the Cosmic Christ.[92]

Mark spoke of the seed of light within us all and told us we could contact that essence even when the light is no longer there. Elizabeth Clare Prophet also taught this:

> Somewhere, sometime in the beginning, God placed a point of light and a seed of light in each one. And you can, by the love of the ruby ray—which is a fierce love and a fearless love—contact that point of the original endowment of God. Perhaps even now if you contact that point, even if that endowment has been taken up and is in another octave because the person is evil, you are contacting what was once the inner master.
>
> Hold on to that teaching, because you may have to deal with such an individual. You may have karma with such a one, and the only way

you can deal with the karma is to find that point, that kernel, that seed that remains undefiled, even if it has been withdrawn.[93]

As you hold the highest vision for them, you will give them the best chance to act from their highest Self, and you will also avoid making karma through sending them negativity.

As the ascended master Kuthumi says, "It is not what happens, but your reaction to it." It doesn't matter who they are or what they do. You do not need to know. What matters is how you react.

Strategy of Darkness 26
- **Cause the lightbearers to make karma with one another.**

This is a subtle variation on the divide-and-conquer tactic. The forces of darkness try to get two people to create karma together. The fallen one instigates the struggle between them by working both sides, perhaps by making sure that each one hears gossip about the other. The fallen one then steps out of the picture while they fight. The two knock each other out, so the fallen one does not have to fight either one.

From the perspective of the dark ones, this is a very successful strategy, because it not only keeps these people out of action for this round, but also has ramifications for future cycles. This strategy of setting brother against brother can keep them karmically tied to one another for successive lives.

This strategy was used very artfully by the Illuminati in the French Revolution and is described in *The Path of Self-Transformation*.[94]

Strategy of Light 26
- **Don't fall for it.**
- **Same as those for numbers 15 and 25.**

The strategies of light are the same as those for numbers 15 (p. 71) and 25 (p. 88). Observe yourself, and watch what is happening in your world. If you see yourself getting drawn into these patterns, withdraw your energy, take an objective look at the situation and plot a new course.

If you have a problem with a brother or sister on the Path, try to resolve it—don't let it simmer and grow. Sometimes you will want to approach them directly in a spirit of love and desire to resolve any misunderstandings. At other times you will only be able to put the situation into the flame and move on.

Be especially careful not to accept negative reports about other people that you can't verify. These can become seeds of discord planted by the enemy in your own consciousness. Presume good will, and give all the benefit of the doubt.

Strategy of Darkness 27
- **The mental projection of indispensability**

This strategy is often combined with those of condemnation and belittlement. While projecting condemnation on others, an individual simultaneously sends out the mental projection that he or she is indispensable. The message is, "I'm indispensable. You can't possibly do this without me. You are not smart enough to figure this out. You need me to carry out these plans. You can never figure this out without me." To reinforce this concept they will sometimes create plans and systems that are unnecessarily convoluted and complex.

Strategy of Light 27
- **Remember that no one is indispensable.**

The Great White Brotherhood has said that no one is indispensable. Even the messenger is not indispensable, and she told us so many times. The masters, in fact, have told us that the movement would suffer just as much at your loss as it would at the loss of the messenger.[95]

The fallen ones often maneuver themselves into positions of power. They want to be the right-hand man. They try to become indispensable. The messenger described how this strategy works in a series of lectures on Community that she delivered during Summit University. Much of this teaching dealt with the psychology of the seed of the wicked. In this excerpt, she provides some insights:

> I have noted that the adversaries of the Great White Brotherhood are often those who cling most steadfastly to the messengers or to a center of light. This is ironic but true, because the adversary of the light is the one who must use the light in order to manifest his opposition. The adversary of the Brotherhood has no source of inner light, and, therefore, he must be in the community, is desperate to be in the community and is most desperate to be near the messenger. The adversary is not a worshiper of the light; he is a worshiper of the personality....
>
> We always have this in movements that are sponsored by the Great White Brotherhood, for the adversaries of the members of that Brotherhood who have been around for centuries always appear and try to get closest to the inner flame

and close to the disciples. By their fruits you shall know them....

It is not up to us to judge, but it is up to us to remain on guard and to know that there are cycles, periods, when the adversary can shine with light.

It is written that Satan himself can be transformed into an angel of light,[96] for it is the borrowed and reflected light of the Brotherhood. The appearance of the adversaries may be one of great light, but the moment the aura is turned inside out and their betrayal and conspiracy is manifest, they become totally dark. Then one sees that they never had any light of their own.[97]

She went on to explain that in order to have a Community of the Holy Spirit, one has to be on guard to know what assails the Community. "And who assails it are those who hate the light the most because the only place that they can get the light to do their evil works and betrayal of the light is by warming their shins on the fire and the hearth of the master and the disciple."

Mother has taught that sometimes on the path of discipleship, you have to be willing to "cut off your right hand." This means that you may be obliged to do without the person who has become seemingly indispensable and on whom you have come to rely. She was forced to do this many times over the years when the one who was indispensable was found to have betrayed the light or to have been in the incorrect vibration.

The Brotherhood teaches us not to rely on the human self of anyone, including our own human self or the human self of the messenger. Give glory to God as the doer. The proud ones who consider themselves indispensable are often not as clever as they think or as they appear to be. They often make big mistakes but scramble very quickly to cover themselves and blame someone else.

It has been said that the wisdom of the common man is generally good. The wisdom of the common man can be thought of as common sense or the voice of the Holy Christ Self. God in you and in others can do what needs to be done. Look to the quality of the heart.

Strategy of Darkness 28
- **Karma dodging**

The fallen ones are experts at dodging their karma. They avoid their karma or get others to bear their karma for them. There are many variations on this theme. They may get you or someone else to handle a situation they should be handling. You may be left paying the bill one way or another: perhaps literally, as in opening your wallet, or maybe through a siphoning of your energy. They get you to do their work. Just when you are about to confront them about a situation, they skip town or simply avoid the meeting where the situation will be handled. They often cry or plead and get themselves off the hook by using the ploy of sympathy. The messenger teaches:

> The Sadducees, the Pharisees, the scribes, the legalists are karma dodgers. They dodge their karma. By milking the people of light, they set up an aura of sanctity and holiness around themselves. They set up around themselves a protection that is not the protection of God but is the energy they have stolen from the people. Look at the tremendous empires built up by the capitalists who have abused our system with their monop-

olies and their manipulations. Their protection is the money of the people. They are using the energy of people as money to protect themselves from their own impending karma. Other people set up energy, other people set up a personality cult.[98]

The messenger gives us a clear example of karma dodging by Caiaphas, who engineered the death of Jesus while getting the people to volunteer to bear the karma for the act:

> Caiaphas says, "It is expedient that one man should die for the people."[99] But what happens? They manipulate the whole thing.... The very magnetism of these black magicians! They knew exactly what they were doing! They succeeded in justifying the death of Jesus Christ in the eyes of the people, and the people cried out, "His blood be upon us and upon our children,"[100] which is to say, "The karma for this deed be on us and our children. We want him dead so much we will take full accountability for his death." That was a karma-dodging act of Caiaphas and all of the rabbis.
>
> So, they get the little people to take accountability. They convince them that something should be done, and then they get them to vote for it.[101]

Strategy of Light 28
- Set loving boundaries, and don't get caught in sympathy.

Be objective. You need to be very clear about what is your duty and what is not. Set loving boundaries in your work and in your personal life. Be careful not to get caught in sympathy. Make the calls that karma dodging not take place, that the fallen ones be unable to dodge their karma. Be willing to face issues lovingly and openly, and yet draw the line when necessary.

Don't be a karma dodger yourself. Take responsibility for your own karma and your own decisions and choices in life. The fallen ones do not take accountability. But the sons and daughters of God do take accountability for their decisions and actions, their thoughts and feelings, their words and deeds.

Strategy of Darkness 29
- **Delay, indecision and procrastination**

Delay, indecision and procrastination are classic strategies of the forces of darkness. The Brotherhood has spoken about the disease of procrastination many times. We see it at work in many areas, including on the world scene. The more important the outcome of a project or plan to the timetables of the Brotherhood, the more damaging is the effect of delay.

The force will therefore attempt to drag out a situation or a project or a decision. Their aim is to get you or others to never reach a decision or complete a project. This can be done in a variety of ways.

One way is to keep researching, planning, studying alternatives, observing the situation and postponing a decision until, finally, important timelines are missed. The delay causes you to miss the wave or the tide of energy from the Brotherhood. The ship is then left high and dry to wait until the next tide comes. Some cycles can be missed altogether.

Another way is to make everything seem more complex than it really is. When faced with a difficult and complex situation, you may feel or be made to feel incapable either of making a decision or of making the best possible decision. So a decision is not made. Other strategies are at work here, too—belittlement, intimidation. The fallen ones try to impress on those who must make decisions: "You are not able to make this kind of decision. It should be left to the indispensable ones with the 'greater attainment.' "

Fear and anxiety in our own consciousness can make us vulnerable to this strategy. This includes the fear of making a mistake or a wrong decision.

The opposite of procrastination is rushing to make a decision without doing the necessary research or planning for the project to be successful.

Strategy of Light 29
- **Move with the cycles, and don't procrastinate.**

Morya says, "Procrastination is a disease that is the death of the disciple." The messenger taught about procrastination in another lecture in the series on Community:

> Whatever is the priority, do it now, not tomorrow. Do it right now. Get it done. And this is that flame of action.
>
> The force will trick you into planning and planning and planning—constantly getting ready to do something. All of these little projects are supposed to lead you to the ultimate goal, but the ultimate goal keeps receding. And you never quite get to the goal because you are always involved in

some little interim project that's not getting you there. This is an amazing phenomenon, but I have watched it happen. I've watched myself slip into this, where I'll get involved in publishing something or working on something that's not going to get out within the next month or the next year. Then Mark would come along and say, "This has to be done now and this is the deadline and this is when I want it."

He would put everybody in motion, and I couldn't spread out my space. I had to conserve my space and my time. The job had to be done now. I work well under that kind of tension and pressure—and I use both words positively. To me, tension and pressure are constructive ingredients in the creative process. Without a set date, you will not demand the maximum energies from God, and therefore, your work will not have the full summoning of forces to spark your creativity.

Therefore, you need to operate under tension and pressure. It makes you summon resources. It makes you develop your mind. It makes you develop your energy, and it keeps you completely involved in the creative process. If you have an eternity to do something, you will never do it. If you think a project can wait five years, the five years will constantly be pushed back.

Please remember this. Wherever you go, postponement is a great temptation, even if it's postponement in the name of service.[102]

Morya, the master of action, says, "When you think of it, do it!" Keep the focus on the priorities, and attend to them first. Prioritize and be willing to make decisions quickly and effectively. When there was hesitation over signing the Declaration of Independence, Saint Germain appeared and commanded: "Sign that document!"[103] Just make a decision!

People are afraid of making the wrong decision, but often the greater error is not making a decision at all. Not making a decision is also a decision by default—it's a decision to do nothing, which can have serious consequences if a danger is not averted or a cycle of opportunity is missed. Remember: don't get entangled in the strategy that stipulates all must be perfect. The decision or the plan or the project does not have to be perfect.

Sometimes the need is simply to take action, break ground and make a decision, even if it is not 100 percent perfect. If you are heading generally in the right direction, you can make midcourse corrections if necessary. Call upon the sponsorship of the masters, do the best you can and follow your heart in all decisions that you make.

Do not procrastinate or delay the cycles of light. Be sure to catch the wave or the tide of light. Be ready to move when Morya calls. Be obedient to your Holy Christ Self. We have all known those times when we felt a sense of urgency. We either moved with it and reaped the rewards or did not move and suffered the consequences. Your Christ Self knows the cycles and will prompt you when you need to move in order to catch a cycle. Do not ignore the promptings.

When Joseph received the warning in a dream to take Mary and Jesus to Egypt, he took them "when he arose."[104] It wasn't the time to plan the trip—where they would stay, how they would earn a living and all the other things they could have spent weeks working out. It was the time to make the trip.

Morya tells us, "You cannot have or be on the path of initiation if you have procrastination, because you don't have the sense of the *now* and fullness of the *now*."[105]

Simplify whenever possible. Morya says, "It is needed to be able to replace a complicated plan with a simpler one—never the reverse—for Our adversaries act from the simple to the complex."[106]

Of course, sometimes caution is appropriate, and we need to remember Morya's admonition: "Don't move till an elephant steps on your foot." We need to do our homework and not be impulsive or rash, hoping that the masters will bail us out if we make a mistake.

The important thing is to be in tune with God's cycles and not let our own dweller-on-the-threshold or any external force trick us into either delay or rash action. Let us be guided by the advice Saint Germain offers us in one of his Shakespearean plays:

> There is a tide in the affairs of men
> Which taken at the flood, leads on to fortune;
> Omitted, all the voyage of their life
> Is bound in shallows and in miseries.[107]

Strategy of Darkness 30
- "Messing with your mind"—psychological dislocation

The aim of the forces of darkness is to "mess with your mind." The battle is won in your mind. If you can stay tethered to God, they cannot win. They are expert at trying to create a state of psychological dislocation. They try to throw you off balance. They make you feel disorganized. They try to make you feel demoralized. All this is designed to induce a state of helplessness.

You then begin to feel that you are in a pressure cooker. They use situations in various aspects of your life to accentuate this feeling and then use other strategies to increase the pressure or the sense of being trapped.

The forces of darkness will often throw different tests at you all at once and use a combination of other strategies. The aim is to keep you off balance, always reacting to external forces and disconnected from the center of being. Eventually, you can get to a point where you can no longer even perceive or respond to different threats because it seems as if threats are coming from every side.

Strategy of Light 30

- **Seal your mind and aura.**

Return to first principles—first things first. Take a deep breath, and center in the heart. Seal the aura and the mind, still the mental and emotional bodies. Reinforce the tube of light by giving the decree to establish the tube of light, either the short or long version. Be the peace-commanding presence in a vortex of calamity and activity.[108]

Saint Germain gives some very practical instruction on passing these kinds of tests in his dictation "May You Pass Every Test!" He says:

> Often it is a matter of stance. How do you hold yourself? Are you in readiness for the next delivery of God or thrust of the sinister force, or are you, as they say these days, "laid-back"? If you slouch, if you are laid-back, wide open, lounging around—the TV set is on, the ads are bombarding their rock beat, the cat is meowing, the dog is barking, the children are screaming, the phone is ringing—how do you expect, then, to keep your

> cool? It is a setup, but you have allowed it.
>
> Now, you can maintain your calm in the midst of these things, but not with a laid-back attitude, for any moment the potatoes on the stove will burn, and everyone will be in an argument, and if you don't watch out, yourself included. And then what have we accomplished? —a lost hour for Saint Germain and the vital work of Helios and Vesta; your own sense, "I will never become a good chela. I will never master my life."
>
> But, beloved ones, it's a matter of one, two, three, four, five—a few simple requirements: Do not allow the family to be bombarded from all directions. Do not allow all these things to be taking place at once. Strive for communion with the heart. Feed the cat, put out the dog, turn off the TV set, make sure all is safe on the stove, and enjoy that circle of communion with God-determination that each member of your family or household or friends shall have the opportunity, by your loving presence, to express something very important from the heart.[109]

Maitreya, the great initiator, says to expect the unexpected:

> I am always watching for the soul who is ready to be initiated in the unexpected. This requires flexibility, being accustomed to the wind of the Holy Spirit blowing to and fro, rearranging the garment of mercy, requiring continual adjustment to and, therefore, continual openness to the flame.[110]

Anticipate that unexpected things will happen and try not to be moved by them. When they do happen, try to make the best of it, and take a calm attitude. Try not to be bombarded with too many things at once. Bring in simple strategies that allow you to have a sense of control about the situation.

Stay centered and focused in your heart. Trust in God and God in your fellow man and in yourself. Do your spiritual work. Sometimes it helps to try a new line of approach to a problem.

Strategy of Darkness 31
- **Discouragement, despair, depression**

We have been told that discouragement and despair are big tools of the sinister force. The false hierarchy seeks to impress mankind with a sense of futility. They love it when we enter into a sense of depression and despair, for their objective is to get us to give up and stop trying. When we wonder, "How long O Lord?" and then have a doom-and-gloom mentality, we are playing into their hands. Depression can set in and reinforce the downward spiral.

Strategy of Light 31
- **Victory consciousness**

In these days we do not need to ask, "How long O Lord?" for the cycles are shortened for the elect. Nevertheless, the messenger once told us that it helps to imagine that there is not long to go until the victory. Do not see yourself under a mountain of karma. Imagine instead that you are in a cosmic egg, and with one mighty burst of energy, you can break through the shell of your karma into the light of the new day.

Do not succumb to despair, depression or discouragement, no matter how bad things look. At any moment the tide can turn, and God can have a victory. Have, therefore, a sense of victory in all that you do, and develop the victory consciousness. Learn to catch yourself as you are going into a downward spiral—or, even better, catch yourself before you enter that spiral. Reverse the negative spirals, and turn them into positive ones.

Claim your victory! Use the Victory calls, decrees 22.02–22.06.[111] Listen to Mark's lecture, "The Majestic Sense of Victory."[112]

Strategy of Darkness 32
- **The pressure to "just give up"**

We are nearing the finish line. The strategy now is to get you to quit before you win the race and win the prize. The dark ones don't want you to finish the race, because they will then win by default. They get you to drop out of the race by employing various clever tactics. A favorite technique is to get you disgusted with them and their strategies so that you give up and simply leave the arena. Then they win. It is as simple as that. All it takes for the dark ones to win is for good people to give up.

We see this strategy being utilized in many ways and in many areas of life. More and more, people want to withdraw from the process—whether it is right action in their job or community, public service of some sort or even the game of life itself. People get fed up with what they see, the politics and unpleasantness they have to deal with, and they withdraw. This strategy is particularly aimed at young people, although any of us can be affected by it.

Strategies of Light 32

- **Don't give up.**

Just don't give up. Make a conscious decision to stick it out, by the grace of God. Do not yield an inch of ground. As the messenger has said:

> You can't quit a situation or a job just because everyone around you is corrupt or faithless. You stay and you stay again because God is testing your staying power, your faith in him that through you he will work a wonder. You build an altar in the midst of the most trying and mundane situation. Build it in your heart. Dedicate every employee, everyone in your company, wherever you work, dedicate them to the will of God. And demand alchemy, transmutation, and give your son, your only son, upon that altar—the Son of God in you.
>
> Be willing to lay down your life for the saving of that situation, that point in city government, that place in Washington where you work. Don't leave because you are in protest of the fallen ones. Stay until you have the victory over them, until you have built your altar, seen the flame and know that those who are to be judged will be judged and those who are of the light will be cut free to do their work. And when you see that that has come, then you may go on to a higher calling.[113]

This also takes discernment. As the masters have told us, there is a time to raise your hands and call for the stopping of the avalanche, and there is also a time to get out of the way!

Develop the victory consciousness. Call to Mighty Victory and the Great Teams of Conquerors. Do not be fooled by outer appearances. Things may not be as bleak as they seem or as the forces of darkness would love to have you believe. We have the Inner Retreat, Maitreya's Mystery School, the mantles of the messenger and the presence and light of the ascended masters with us.

Remember the decree, "The Flame of Freedom Speaks": "I will never give up, I will never turn back, I will never submit." Why not give it now with the full fervor of your heart? Say it right now into the teeth of every problem or burden that besets you and your loved ones:

The Flame of Freedom Speaks
by Saint Germain

The Flame of Freedom speaks—the Flame of Freedom within each heart. The Flame of Freedom saith unto all: Come apart now and be a separate and chosen people, elect unto God—men who have chosen their election well, who have determined to cast their lot in with the immortals. These are they who have set their teeth with determination, who have said:

I will never give up
I will never turn back
I will never submit
I will bear the flame of freedom unto my victory
I will bear this flame in honor
I will sustain the glory of life within my nation
I will sustain the glory of life within my being
I will win my ascension
I will forsake all idols and

I will forsake the idol of my outer self
I will have the glory of my immaculate divinely
 conceived Self manifesting within me
I AM freedom and
I AM determined to be freedom
I AM the flame of freedom and
I AM determined to bear it to all
I AM God's freedom and he is indeed free
I AM freed by his power and his power is supreme
I AM fulfilling the purposes of God's kingdom

Endurance is a quality that Morya teaches and Saint Germain admires. Morya talks about staying power, the ability to hang on, which can be your greatest asset on the path of initiation at certain times of trial. Simply hang on. And when the morning comes, you find the joy of the risen Christ. And the morning *will* come, and it comes *more quickly than you think!*[114]

Strategy of Darkness 33
- **Preempt the Brotherhood's moves**

The false hierarchy loves to jump the gun, to preempt the moves of the Brotherhood of light. The false guru or teacher comes before the true guru appears, to try to take you off the path to your ascension. You also find that the false hierarchy impostor of the twin flame comes before the true twin flame appears.

Strategy of the Light 33
- **Anticipate the moves of the dark ones, and expect the initiation.**

Watch for the preempting of your plans for the Brotherhood, and do not be caught off guard. Expect the unexpected. Make the calls to consume or reverse or collapse the strategies that oppose your victory. Call for the binding of the backlash to the light that is released when you have a thrust of light for the right. Remember that God allows us to be tested. And just as God has a right to test us, Morya says that we have a right to pass our tests.[115]

Conclusion

Morya has told us that the fallen ones serve up the same old plots year after year, century after century. Their tapes are so old, but they work so well they do not need to create new ones.[116] Their ploys come in many disguises. Mark tells us: "You all have a great deal to learn about the wiles of Satan. The wiles of Satan are many. They come in many disguises and many brands. It reminds me of a box of chocolates, real goodies with all kinds of different coatings on them, sugar and spice and everything nice—till you get inside."[117]

But through the sacred labor of the messengers, some of these strategies now stand exposed, and the corresponding spiritual antidotes have been provided. And remember the words of Mother Mary: the key to deciphering the code of the spiritual wisdom God would impart to us has been placed in the aura of the messenger.[118]

And our dear Mother of the Flame has told us that when she ascends, millions of fallen ones will go to their judgment, and millions of lightbearers will be cut free to take up the Teachings of the Ascended Masters!

The final word is from Saint Germain from his address, "May You Pass Every Test!" published in *Lords of the Seven Rays*.

> Let us expand consciousness now. Let us increase the circle of the aura. Let us realize that

we are not these lower bodies, but we are God-free beings using these vehicles to accomplish an end.[119]

The master invites us to realize our identity in God, our birthright of freedom, and asks us to move forward into the arms of God, no matter the challenges. But we will not be alone in taking that step.

> When you decide it is *done*, and you decide with the full power of your I AM Presence that you are willing to *wrestle* with the old momentum and not allow that beast to rise from the dead at any time, when you will *plunge* the sword of the Word, and the *spoken Word*, into it, when you will wrestle with every temptation to breathe upon it the breath of life again and take it up again—I tell you, beloved ones, so many angels will come to assist you that as you walk the earth, it will be as though a cloud of glory surrounded you—so many angels will come to reinforce the determination of the sons and daughters of God to be free.[120]

0.10   Count-to-Nine Decree
by Cuzco

In the name of the beloved mighty victorious Presence of God, I AM in me, my very own beloved Holy Christ Self, beloved Archangel Michael, Prince Oromasis, Mighty Astrea, Goddess of Light, beloved Ascended Master Cuzco, beloved Lanello, the entire Spirit of the Great White Brotherhood and the World Mother, elemental life—fire, air, water, and earth! I decree:

Come now by love divine,
Guard thou this soul of mine,
Make now my world all thine,
God's light around me shine.

I count one,
It is done.
O feeling world, Be still!
Two and three,
I AM free,
Peace, it is God's will.

I count four,
I do adore
My Presence all divine.
Five and six,
O God, affix
My gaze on thee sublime!

I count seven,
Come, O Heaven,
My energies take hold!
Eight and nine,
Completely thine,
My mental world enfold!

> The white fire light now encircles me,
> All riptides are rejected!
> With God's own might around me bright
> I AM by love protected!

I accept this done right now with full power! I AM this done right now with full power! I AM, I AM, I AM God-life expressing perfection all ways at all times. This which I call forth for myself I call forth for every man, woman, and child on this planet!

10.14   Decree to Beloved Mighty Astrea

In the name of the beloved mighty victorious Presence of God, I AM in me, mighty I AM Presence and Holy Christ Selves of Keepers of the Flame, lightbearers of the world and all who are to ascend in this life, by and through the magnetic power of the sacred fire vested in the threefold flame burning within my heart, I call to beloved Mighty Astrea and Purity, Archangel Gabriel and Hope, beloved Serapis Bey and the seraphim and cherubim of God, beloved Lanello, the entire Spirit of the Great White Brotherhood and the World Mother, elemental life—fire, air, water, and earth! to lock your cosmic circles and swords of blue flame in, through, and around:

Insert 1:   my four lower bodies, my electronic belt, my heart chakra and all of my chakras, my entire consciousness, being, and world.

Cut me loose and set me free (3x) from all that is less than God's perfection and my own divine plan fulfilled.

1. O beloved Astrea, may God purity
   Manifest here for all to see,
   God's divine will shining through
   Circle and sword of brightest blue.

First chorus: Come now answer this my call
Lock thy circle round us all.
Circle and sword of brightest blue,
Blaze now, raise now, shine right through!

2. Cutting life free from patterns unwise,
   Burdens fall off while souls arise
   Into thine arms of infinite love,
   Merciful shining from heaven above.

3. Circle and sword of Astrea now shine,
   Blazing blue-white my being refine,
   Stripping away all doubt and fear,
   Faith and goodwill patterns appear.

Second chorus: Come now answer this my call,
Lock thy circle round us all.
Circle and sword of brightest blue,
Raise our youth now, blaze right through!

Third chorus: Come now answer this my call,
Lock thy circle round us all.
Circle and sword of brightest blue,
Raise mankind now, shine right through!

And in full faith I consciously accept this manifest, manifest, manifest! (3x) right here and now with full power, eternally sustained, all powerfully active, ever expanding, and world enfolding until all are wholly ascended in the light and free! Beloved I AM! Beloved I AM! Beloved I AM!

20.09 "I Cast Out the Dweller-On-the-Threshold!"
by Jesus Christ

In the name I AM THAT I AM Elohim,
     Saint Germain, Portia, Guru Ma, Lanello,
Padma Sambhava, Kuan Yin and the Five Dhyani Buddhas
In the name I AM THAT I AM Sanat Kumara,
     Gautama Buddha, Lord Maitreya, Jesus Christ,
Om Vairochana • Akshobhya • Ratnasambhava
     Amitabha • Amoghasiddhi • Vajrasattva Om
I cast out the dweller-on-the-threshold of _____

In the name of my beloved mighty I AM Presence and Holy Christ Self, Archangel Michael and the hosts of the Lord, in the name Jesus Christ, I challenge the personal and planetary dweller-on-the-threshold, and I say:

You have no power over me! *You* may not threaten or mar the face of my God within my soul. *You* may not taunt or tempt me with past or present or future, for I AM hid with Christ in God. I AM his bride. I AM accepted by the Lord.

You have no power to destroy me!

Therefore, be *bound!* by the Lord himself.

Your day is *done!* You may no longer inhabit this temple.

In the name I AM THAT I AM, be *bound!* you tempter of my soul. Be *bound!* you point of pride of the original fall of the fallen ones! You have no power, no reality, no worth. You occupy no time or space of my being.

You have no power in my temple. You may no longer steal the light of my chakras. You may not steal the light of my heart flame or my I AM Presence.

Be *bound!* then, O Serpent and his seed and all implants of the sinister force, for *I AM THAT I AM!*

I AM the Son of God this day, and I occupy this temple fully and wholly until the coming of the Lord, until the

New Day, until all be fulfilled, and until this generation of the seed of Serpent pass away.

Burn through, O living Word of God!

By the power of Brahma, Vishnu, and Shiva, in the name Brahman: I AM THAT I AM and I stand and I cast out the dweller.

Let him be bound by the power of the LORD's host! Let him be consigned to the flame of the sacred fire of Alpha and Omega, that that one may not go out to tempt the innocent and the babes in Christ.

Blaze the power of Elohim!

Elohim of God—Elohim of God—Elohim of God

Descend now in answer to my call. As the mandate of the LORD—as Above, so below—occupy now.

Bind the fallen self! *Bind* the synthetic self! Be *out* then!

Bind the fallen one! For there is no more remnant or residue in my life of any, or any part of that one.

Lo, I AM, in Jesus' name, the victor over Death and Hell! (2x)

Lo, I AM THAT I AM in me—in the name of Jesus Christ—is *here and now* the victor over Death and Hell!

Lo! it is done.

50.05 Beloved Cyclopea, Beholder of Perfection

Beloved mighty victorious Presence of God, I AM in me, Holy Christ Selves of all earth's evolutions, beloved Cyclopea and Virginia, beloved Helios and Vesta, Lanello and K 17, the entire Spirit of the Great White Brotherhood and the World Mother, elemental life—fire, air, water, and earth! In the name of the beloved Presence of God which I AM and by and through the magnetic power of the sacred fire vested in the threefold flame burning within my heart, I decree:

1. Beloved Cyclopea,
   Thou Beholder of Perfection,
   Release to us thy divine direction,
   Clear our way from all debris,
   Hold the immaculate thought for me

Refrain: I AM, I AM beholding All,
   Mine eye is single as I call;
   Raise me now and set me free,
   Thy holy image now to be.

2. Beloved Cyclopea,
   Thou Enfolder All Seeing,
   Mold in light my very being,
   Purify my thought and feeling,
   Hold secure God's Law appealing.

3. Beloved Cyclopea,
   Radiant Eye of Ancient Grace,
   By God's hand his Image trace
   On the fabric of my soul,
   Erase all bane and keep me whole.

4. Beloved Cyclopea,
   Guard for aye the City Foursquare,
   Hear and implement my prayer,
   Trumpet my victory on the air,
   Hold the purity of truth so fair.

And in full faith I consciously accept this manifest, manifest, manifest! (3x) right here and now with full power, eternally sustained, all-powerfully active, ever expanding, and world enfolding until all are wholly ascended in the light and free! Beloved I AM! Beloved I AM! Beloved I AM!

The Chart of Your Divine Self

The Chart of Your Divine Self is a portrait of you and of the God within you. It is a diagram of you and your potential to become who you really are. It is an outline of your spiritual anatomy.

The upper figure is your "I AM Presence," the Presence of God that is individualized in each one of us. It is your personalized "I AM THAT I AM." Your I AM Presence is surrounded by seven concentric spheres of spiritual energy that make up what is called your "Causal Body." The spheres of pulsating energy contain the record of the good works you have performed since your very first incarnation on earth. They are like your cosmic bank account.

The middle figure in the chart represents the "Holy Christ Self," who is also called the Higher Self. You can think of your Holy Christ Self as your chief guardian angel and dearest friend, your inner teacher and voice of conscience. Just as the I AM Presence is the presence of God that is individualized for each of us, so the Holy Christ Self is the presence of the Universal Christ that is individualized for each of us. "The Christ" is actually a title given to those who have attained oneness with their Higher Self, or Christ Self. That is why Jesus was called "Jesus, the Christ."

What the Chart shows is that each of us has a Higher Self, or "Inner Christ," and that each of us is destined to become one with that Higher Self—whether we call it the

The Chart of Your Divine Self

Christ, the Buddha, the Tao or the Atman. This "Inner Christ" is what the Christian mystics sometimes refer to as the "inner man of the heart," and what the Upanishads mysteriously describe as a being the "size of a thumb" who "dwells deep within the heart."

We all have moments when we feel that connection with our Higher Self—when we are creative, loving, joyful. But there are other moments when we feel out of sync with our Higher Self—moments when we become angry, depressed, lost. What the spiritual path is all about is learning to sustain the connection to the higher part of ourselves so that we can make our greatest contribution to humanity.

The shaft of white light descending from the I AM Presence through the Holy Christ Self to the lower figure in the Chart is the crystal cord (sometimes called the silver cord). It is the "umbilical cord," the lifeline, that ties you to Spirit.

Your crystal cord also nourishes that special, radiant Flame of God that is ensconced in the secret chamber of your heart. It is called the threefold flame, or divine spark, because it is literally a spark of sacred fire that God has transmitted from his heart to yours. This flame is called "threefold" because it engenders the primary attributes of Spirit—power, wisdom and love.

The mystics of the world's religions have contacted the divine spark, describing it as the seed of divinity within. Buddhists, for instance, speak of the "germ of Buddhahood" that exists in every living being. In the Hindu tradition, the Katha Upanishad speaks of the "light of the Spirit" that is concealed in the "secret high place of the heart" of all beings.

Likewise, the fourteenth-century Christian theologian

and mystic Meister Eckhart teaches of the divine spark when he says, "God's seed is within us."

When we decree, we meditate on the flame in the secret chamber of our heart. This secret chamber is your own private meditation room, your interior castle, as Teresa of Avila called it. In Hindu tradition, the devotee visualizes a jeweled island in his heart. There he sees himself before a beautiful altar, where he worships his teacher in deep meditation.

Jesus spoke of entering the secret chamber of the heart when he said: "When thou prayest, enter into thy closet, and when thou hast shut thy door, pray to thy Father which is in secret; and thy Father which seeth in secret shall reward thee openly."

The lower figure in the Chart of Your Divine Self represents you on the spiritual path, surrounded by the violet flame and the protective white light of God. The soul is the living potential of God—the part of you that is mortal but that can become immortal.

The purpose of your soul's evolution on earth is to grow in self-mastery, balance your karma and fulfill your mission on earth so that you can return to the spiritual dimensions that are your real home. When your soul at last takes flight and ascends back to God and the heaven-world, you will become an ascended master, free from the rounds of karma and rebirth. The high-frequency energy of the violet flame can help you reach that goal more quickly.

Notes

All books referenced here are published by Summit University Press unless otherwise noted.

1. Lord Maitreya, "Find Your Way Back to Me," July 2, 1978, published in *Pearls of Wisdom*, August 13 & 20, 2000.
2. For more information about the dweller-on-the-threshold, see Mark L. Prophet and Elizabeth Clare Prophet, *The Enemy Within: Encountering and Conquering the Dark Side*.
3. Profile Brochure, back cover.
4. Archeia Mary, *Pearls of Wisdom*, November 2, 1975.
5. Mark Prophet, staff meeting, "Houses of Light and Houses of Darkness," January 14, 1973.
6. For the Messenger's teaching on angels of light and fallen angels, see Elizabeth Clare Prophet, *Fallen Angels and the Origins of Evil*.
7. Lord Maitreya, "Find Your Way Back to Me," July 2, 1978, published in *Pearls of Wisdom*, August 13 & 20, 2000.
8. Ibid.
9. Lord Maitreya, November 22, 1976.
10. Elizabeth Clare Prophet, Summit University lecture, "Studies of the Human Aura #2," April 16, 1975.
11. Decree 70.00, "I AM the One," by Saint Germain.
12. John 8:32.
13. Saint Germain, "The Harvest," December 2, 1984, published in *Pearls of Wisdom*, December 23, 1984.
14. Matt. 13:24–30, 36–43.
15. Elizabeth Clare Prophet, "The Personal and Planetary Initiations of the Crucifixion of Christ," March 23, 1978, published in cassette album *The Second Coming of Christ—Album I*.
16. Mark Prophet, staff meeting, November 9, 1968.
17. Mark Prophet, Friday evening service, January 21, 1972.
18. Mark Prophet, staff meeting, May 25, 1969.
19. Elizabeth Clare Prophet, Summit University lecture, December 3, 1973.
20. Lord Maitreya, "Find Your Way Back to Me," July 2, 1978,

published in *Pearls of Wisdom*, August 13 & 20, 2000.
21 Elizabeth Clare Prophet, Summit University lecture, September 27, 1973.
22 Saint Germain, "The Sword of Your Attention Is the Gate to Mastery," December 8, 1963, published in *Pearls of Wisdom*, July 4 & 11, 1976.
23 Mark L. Prophet and Elizabeth Clare Prophet, *Lords of the Seven Rays*, book 2, p. 271.
24 Elizabeth Clare Prophet, "The Seventh Commandment: Thou Shalt Not Commit Adultery," May 16, 1982, published in cassette album A8239.
25 Ps. 82:6.
26 Mother Mary, "The Re-Creation of Self," August 13, 1989, published in *Pearls of Wisdom*, October 29, 1989.
27 Kuthumi, "Remember the Ancient Encounter," January 27, 1985, published in *Pearls of Wisdom*, March 3, 1985, p. 82.
28 Elizabeth Clare Prophet, Saint Germain service, August 3, 1991.
29 See Elizabeth Clare Prophet, *Predict Your Future: Understand the Cycles of the Cosmic Clock.*
30 Elizabeth Clare Prophet, Summit University lecture, December 3, 1973.
31 Lady Master Leto, January 2, 1972.
32 Elizabeth Clare Prophet, August 7, 1994, published on cassette B94097.
33 Mark Prophet, staff meeting, December 14, 1970.
34 Rev. 12:10.
35 Elizabeth Clare Prophet, "Physician, Heal Thyself!" May 25, 1983, published in cassette album A83143.
36 Elizabeth Clare Prophet, "Teachings of the Cosmic Christ #1," January 8, 1979, published in *Pearls of Wisdom*, September 24, 2000.
37 John 3:17.
38 *Lords of the Seven Rays*, book two, p. 256.
39 Elizabeth Clare Prophet, lecture on the embodiments of Saint Germain, July 6, 1984, published in cassette album A84120, *The Flame of Freedom Speaks.*
40 "Teachings of the Cosmic Christ #1."
41 Justina, "The Forgiveness of Eve," January 1, 1978, published in *Pearls of Wisdom*, May 14 & 21, 2000.
42 Elizabeth Clare Prophet, "An Exposé of False Teachings," October 13, 1975, published in cassette album A7544, *Until the New Day.*
43 Mark Prophet, Sunday morning service, February 28, 1971.
44 Elizabeth Clare Prophet, "The Mysteries of the Holy Spirit," August 8, 1978.
45 Elizabeth Clare Prophet, "Religions of the World #11," November

7, 1974.
46 "Teachings of the Cosmic Christ #1."
47 Kuthumi, "Guarding the Souls of Christed Ones for Mission 2001," October 7, 1977, published in cassette album A7800, *Soul Liberation—Album I*.
48 John 14:30.
49 *A Special Dispensation, Book 1*, released by Elizabeth Clare Prophet, pp. 4–5.
50 Mark L. Prophet and Elizabeth Clare Prophet, *Foundations of the Path*, p. 107.
51 "Teachings of the Cosmic Christ #1."
52 Kuthumi, "Remember the Ancient Encounter," January 27, 1985, published in *Pearls of Wisdom*, March 3, 1985.
53 Rev. 11:3.
54 El Morya, "Regarding Your Chelaship: The Equation of Karma," July 7, 1991, published in *Pearls of Wisdom*, September 22, 1991.
55 John 21:22.
56 *Lords of the Seven Rays*, book 2, pp. 268–269.
57 God Meru, "A Scroll from the Library of Our Retreat," December 20, 1973, published in cassette album A7410, *Christmas '73: Mission South America with Mother*.
58 Elizabeth Clare Prophet, *The Great White Brotherhood in the Culture, History and Religion of America*, p. 99.
59 Jesus, "The Day of Thy Christhood," November 1, 1987, published in *Pearls of Wisdom*, December 13, 1987.
60 Saint Germain, "A Victory Celebration: Almighty God Is the Winner," November 5, 1980, published in *Pearls of Wisdom*, November 16, 1980.
61 Sanat Kumara, "The Awakening of the Buddha," January 1, 1983, published in *Pearls of Wisdom*, April 4, 1999.
62 The Garden of Eden was the Mystery School of Lord Maitreya on Lemuria. The Inner Retreat is the location of the Mystery School of Lord Maitreya come again in this age.
63 *Lords of the Seven Rays*, book 2, p. 269.
64 1984 *Pearls of Wisdom, Book One, Introduction I*, p. 2.
65 Rom. 3:4.
66 Mark L. Prophet and Elizabeth Clare Prophet, *The Path of Self-Transformation*, p. 101. These tests are also outlined in lectures by the Messenger from October 8, 1978, published in cassette album A7896, *The Religious Philosophy of Karl Marx: The Economic Philosophy of Jesus Christ*.
67 Elizabeth Clare Prophet, Sunday sermon, February 28, 1982, published on cassette K8222.
68 Elizabeth Clare Prophet, Summit University lecture, "Studies of the Human Aura #3," April 17, 1975.

69 2 Cor. 6:14.
70 Elizabeth Clare Prophet, Summit University lecture, "Teachings of Uriel #7," June 9, 1978.
71 Mark Prophet, lecture to AMU, "Cosmic Law #9," July 15, 1971.
72 Mark Prophet, staff meeting, May 6, 1971.
73 Alexander Gaylord, "The Golden Rule Standard," *Pearls of Wisdom,* June 28, 1970.
74 *The Path of Self-Transformation,* pp. 88–89.
75 Unpublished dictation by Lord Maitreya, 1976, "Maitreya on Meditation" seminar.
76 Elizabeth Clare Prophet, Summit University lecture, "The Era of the Holy Spirit," August 16, 1978.
77 Pallas Athena, *Pearls of Wisdom,* July 7, 1961.
78 *Encyclopedia Britannica,* 1971, q.v. Fabius.
79 Saint Germain, "For the Victory!" July 4, 1992, published in *Pearls of Wisdom,* October 18, 1992.
80 Decrees 22.02–22.06, "Affirmations by Mighty Victory," in *Prayers, Meditations, Dynamic Decrees for the Coming Revolution in Higher Consciousness.*
81 Mark Prophet, staff meeting, October 22, 1970.
82 *Sacred Ritual for Keepers of the Flame,* page 10.
83 Phil. 2:6.
84 Elizabeth Clare Prophet, stump lecture, October 17, 1985.
85 "Call Upon the Lord," Song 525, Part 7, "I Shall Not Be Moved," in *Church Universal and Triumphant Book of Hymns and Songs.* Words from a dictation by Lanello, September 23, 1979.
86 Matt. 7:20.
87 Elizabeth Clare Prophet, "Political Party and Personal Involvement," October 11, 1976.
88 For specific examples and further teaching on this subject, see cassette album A7938, *Mother's Manifesto on the Manipulators of Capitalism and Communism.*
89 Sanat Kumara, "The Summoning of the Servants of God," July 4, 1978, published in *Pearls of Wisdom,* May 16, 1999.
90 Matt. 5:38–45.
91 John 21:22.
92 Elizabeth Clare Prophet, "Eighteen Questions from the Mother of the World," November 27, 1981, published in cassette album A8260, *On the Mother—Album I.*
93 Elizabeth Clare Prophet, "Meeting Your Inner Master," February 7, 1992, published in *Pearls of Wisdom,* July 16, 23 and 30, 2000.
94 *The Path of Self-Transformation,* pp. 77–78.
95 Sanat Kumara, "The Summoning of the Servants of God," July 4, 1978, published in *Pearls of Wisdom,* May 16, 1999.
96 2 Cor. 11:14.

97 Elizabeth Clare Prophet, *Community*, pp. 184, 185.
98 Elizabeth Clare Prophet, "Welcome Address," February 17, 1979.
99 John 18:14.
100 Matt. 27:25.
101 Elizabeth Clare Prophet, Summit University lecture, November 17, 1982, published in cassette album A84016, *Life and Works of Jesus Christ—John the Beloved Seminar*.
102 Elizabeth Clare Prophet, *Community*, pp. 53–54.
103 Saint Germain, "The Grand Adventure," July 4, 1962, published in *Pearls of Wisdom*, August 21 & 28, 1977.
104 Matt. 2:13, 14.
105 Quoted by the Messenger in a lecture to Summit University, "Understanding Yourself #9," February 13, 1975.
106 Nicholas and Helena Roerich, *New Era Community* (New York, N.Y.: Agni Yoga Society, 1951), p. 64.
107 Julius Cæsar. Act iv. Sc. 3.
108 *Lords of the Seven Rays*, book 2, p. 255.
109 Ibid., pp. 258–59.
110 Lord Maitreya, "Expect the Unexpected," December 13, 1975, published in *Pearls of Wisdom*, June 25, 2000.
111 Decrees 22.02–22.06, "Affirmations by Mighty Victory," in *Prayers, Meditations, Dynamic Decrees for the Coming Revolution in Higher Consciousness*.
112 Mark Prophet, "The Majestic Sense of Victory," December 31, 1969, published in *Pearls of Wisdom*, January 2, 2000. Also published in cassette album A86030, *Discourses on Cosmic Law XIII*.
113 Elizabeth Clare Prophet, "Teachings of the Mother on Morya as Abraham," August 27, 1982, published in cassette album A82111, *In the Heart of the Inner Retreat—Album II*.
114 Elizabeth Clare Prophet, Summit University lecture, "Studies of the Human Aura #2," April 16, 1975.
115 Elizabeth Clare Prophet, comments following dictation by El Morya, December 31, 1986, published in *Pearls of Wisdom*, December 28, 1986.
116 El Morya, "To Awaken America to a Vital Purpose," April 16, 1976, published in *Lords of the Seven Rays*, book 2, p. 47.
117 Mark Prophet, May 27, 1967.
118 Archeia Mary, *Pearls of Wisdom*, November 2, 1975.
119 *Lords of the Seven Rays*, book 2, p. 251.
120 Ibid., p. 268.

Acknowledgments

Profound gratitude to Lord Maitreya, Gautama Buddha, Jesus and all the sponsoring masters of Summit University for the wealth of teachings released at Summit University through the messengers.

Gratitude to the messengers, who have given so much of themselves over more than forty years so that we could understand the strategies of light and darkness and have such a clear road map for our return to God.

For More Information

For more information about The Summit Lighthouse Library, to place an order or to receive a free catalog of our books and products, please contact us at:

The Summit Lighthouse Library
PO Box 5000
Gardiner, MT 59030-5000, USA
Tel: 1-800-245-5445 or 406-848-9500
Fax: 1-800-221-8307 or 406-848-9555
www.summituniversitypress.com
info@summituniversitypress.com

For Further Study

If you desire to learn more about the strategies of light and darkness, study the lectures, dictations and teachings of the messengers Mark and Elizabeth Clare Prophet. All that they have taught is to help us win the victory, and their teachings contain the strategies of light to counteract the strategies of darkness, of which they warn us. The following publications are particularly helpful:

1. *Fallen Angels and the Origins of Evil*
2. *The Mechanization Concept*, by the Great Divine Director, teacher of Saint Germain and El Morya; published in *Pearls of Wisdom*, 1965
3. *Mysteries of the Holy Grail*, by Archangel Gabriel
4. *The Path of the Higher Self*, book 1 in the *Climb the Highest Mountain* series
5. *The Path of Self-Transformation*, book 2 in the *Climb the Highest Mountain* series
6. *The Masters and the Spiritual Path*, book 3 in the *Climb the Highest Mountain* series
7. *The Enemy Within: Encountering and Conquering the Dark Side*

The following are also recommended reading:

1. *The Screwtape Letters*, by C. S. Lewis. Letters to a small demon from his hierarch. This book was required reading for Summit University students.
2. *The Art of War*, by Sun Tsu. Mark loved his copy of

this book, and he carried the book around and studied it. Sun Tsu was the greatest strategist of all time. He taught, "Your field of attack is the mind of the opposing general." He also said, "When you are strong, appear to be weak." And is that not what our beloved Mother of the Flame is doing?

You must teach the children of light the strategies of the seed of the wicked in every way: polluting the minds and bodies, hearts and souls, preventing them therefore from having the soundness of mind, the strength of soul and heart and body not only to entertain angels, not only to know the truth of the strong spiritual teachings of the age, but also to wage the warfare of the Spirit with the archangels, joining them daily for the binding of the world forces of tyranny moving into this hemisphere, moving into the mountain of Almighty God.
    Jesus, *Pearls of Wisdom* ~ June 5, 1984

Mark L. Prophet and Elizabeth Clare Prophet are pioneers of modern spirituality and internationally renowned authors. For more than 40 years the Prophets have published the teachings of the immortal saints and sages of East and West known as the ascended masters. Together they have given the world a new understanding of the ancient wisdom as well as a path of practical mysticism.

Their books, available in fine bookstores worldwide, have been translated into 20 languages and are sold in more than 30 countries.

Printed by Libri Plureos GmbH in Hamburg, Germany